The Blackbirch Visual Encyclopedia

High-Tech Science

BLACKBIRCH®
PRESS

THOMSON

GALE

San Diego • Detroit • New York • San Francisco • Cleveland • New Haven, Conn. • Waterville, Maine • London • Munich

Text credit: Christopher Oxlade

Illustration credit: Elisabetta Ferrero, Giuliano Fornari, Lee Montgomery, Steve Noon, Nicki Palin, Sebastian Quigley, Alessandro Rabatti, Colin Rose, Ivan Stalio, Roger Stewart, Thomas Trojer, Alan Weston, Martin Woodward, David Wright

Photograph on page 25: Eye of Science/Science Photo Library; on page 28: Will and Deni Mcintyre/Science Photo Library; on pages 12, 13, 16, 24, 29: The Illustrated London News Picture Library

LIBRARY OF CONGRESS CATALOGING-IN-PUBLICATION DATA

Harris, Nicholas, 1956-
High-tech science / Nicholas Harris.
    p. cm. — (Blackbirch visual encyclopedia)
    Summary: A visual encyclopedia of sciences which rely on technology, including electronics, communications, optics, energy, and transportation.
    ISBN 1-56711-522-5 (lib. bdg. : alk. paper)
    1. Technology—Juvenile literature. 2. Science—Juvenile literature. [1. Technology—Encyclopedias. 2. Science—Encyclopedias.] I. Series.
T48.H385 2002
603—dc21   2002018661

Printed in Singapore
10 9 8 7 6 5 4 3 2 1

CONTENTS

ELECTRONICS

ELECTRONS are tiny particles that are parts of atoms. An electric current is a flow of electrons. Electronics is the study of how electrons behave and how they can be controlled so that they can do useful jobs. Nearly all the machines we use in our everyday lives—from radios, calculators, and television remote controls to telephones, computers, and cars—contain electronic circuits that make them work. Electronics are especially important in information technology *(see page 9)* and communications *(see page 12)*.

A thermionic triode valve was designed to amplify (strengthen) electric signals. A central electrode is heated inside a glass tube. Electrons flow from it to another, outer electrode. A small electric signal causes large changes to this electron flow, producing a more powerful electric signal.

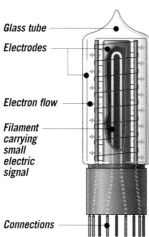

Glass tube

Electrodes

Electron flow

Filament carrying small electric signal

Connections

The study of electronics began at the end of the 19th century, and had its first practical use in the early 20th century in the development of radio communications *(see page 16)*. The first electronic devices were called thermionic valves. These included the diode valve, which allowed current to flow through it one way but not the other, and the triode *(above)*, in which a small current could be used to control a much larger current. The parts of thermionic valves, some of which glowed red hot, had to be enclosed in a glass tube with the air removed to create a vacuum.

In the 1950s valves were quickly replaced by semiconductor devices. A semiconductor is a material that can act as both a good conductor of electricity and an insulator. Semiconductor devices are much simpler, smaller and more reliable than valves.

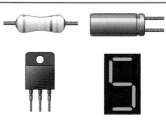

Examples of electronic components: *(clockwise, from top left)* resistor, capacitor, light-emitting diode, and transistor. The metal legs connect them to the circuit.

There are dozens of different electronic components, but the most common ones are resistors, capacitors, diodes, and transistors. A resistor restricts the flow of current in a circuit. Capacitors store electric charge. Current can flow into them until they are full, and out of them until they are empty. A diode allows current to flow one way but not the other. A transistor can act as a switch or an amplifier. It has three connections. The current flowing between two connections is controlled by a tiny current flowing into the third.

An electronic circuit is made up of components linked together by wires around which an electric current flows. By combining different components and connecting them in different ways, it is possible to make electronic circuits which do almost any job. In an electronic circuit, the components of the circuit itself control the current. For example, in a security light, the electric current is turned on or off by an electronic device that detects whether it is dark and whether anybody is moving nearby.

Electronic calculators, personal computers, and hi-fi systems all contain complex electronic circuits that control how they work.

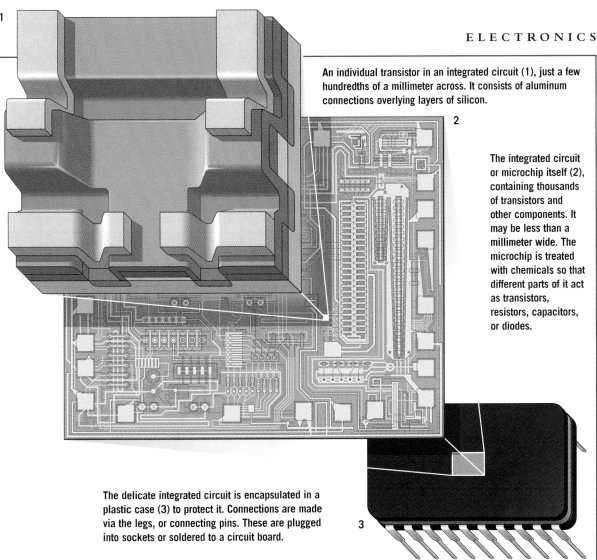

An individual transistor in an integrated circuit (1), just a few hundredths of a millimeter across. It consists of aluminum connections overlying layers of silicon.

2

The integrated circuit or microchip itself (2), containing thousands of transistors and other components. It may be less than a millimeter wide. The microchip is treated with chemicals so that different parts of it act as transistors, resistors, capacitors, or diodes.

The delicate integrated circuit is encapsulated in a plastic case (3) to protect it. Connections are made via the legs, or connecting pins. These are plugged into sockets or soldered to a circuit board.

3

INTEGRATED CIRCUITS

Single electronic components are normally soldered (connected by metal) onto a circuit board by their legs. Metal tracks on the board connect the components together. Circuits that require hundreds or thousands of components would be enormous. Modern circuits use integrated circuits, or microchips, in which microscopically small components and the connections between them are built into a wafer of semiconductor material, which is normally silicon. This is why integrated circuits are often called silicon chips. There are thousands of different integrated circuits. Some, such as amplifier chips or timing chips, contain a few dozen components. Others, such as computer processors or memory chips, contain hundreds of thousands or even millions.

The first integrated circuit was built in 1959 in the United States by Texas Instruments. Since then the number of components that can be fitted onto a chip has increased rapidly. An integrated circuit starts life as thin wafer of semiconductor material. The components are built into it by adding and removing layers of semiconductor material, conductors, and insulators, using complex chemical and photographic processes.

An ant holding an integrated circuit containing hundreds of components.

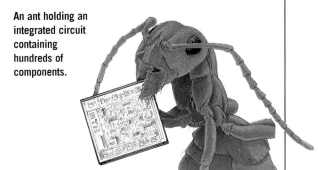

DIGITAL ELECTRONICS

IN MANY ELECTRONIC circuits, such as those in radios, the current can be of any strength. These circuits are called analog circuits. In digital circuits, the current can have only two strengths—on and off. Digital circuits are used in devices in which the flow of electricity represents information, such as computers.

Numbers are represented in digital circuits using the binary number system. This uses only the digits 0 and 1 and so can easily be represented in electronic circuits by turning currents on or off. In the decimal system (numbers we use in everyday life: 1, 2, 3, etc.), the digits of a number represent ones, tens, hundreds, and so on. In the binary system *(see illustration below left)*, the digits represent ones, twos, fours, eights and so on. In digital circuits, each 0 or 1 is called a bit. A four-bit binary "word" can represent decimal numbers up to 15 (one 8, one 4, one 2, and one 1).

BINARY					DECIMAL
16	8	4	2	1	
0	0	0	0	0	0
0	0	0	0	1	1
0	0	0	1	0	2
0	0	0	1	1	3
0	0	1	0	0	4
0	0	1	0	1	5
0	0	1	1	0	6
0	0	1	1	1	7
0	1	0	0	0	8
0	1	0	0	1	9
0	1	0	1	0	10
0	1	0	1	1	11
0	1	1	0	0	12
0	1	1	0	1	13
0	1	1	1	0	14
0	1	1	1	1	15
1	0	0	0	0	16

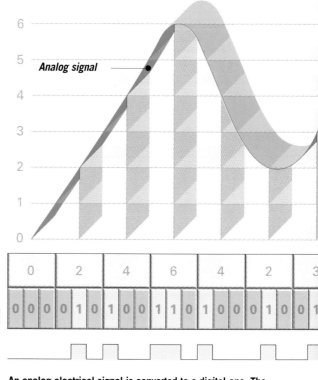

An analog electrical signal is converted to a digital one. The bits become electrical pulses: on (1) or off (0).

Almost any sort of information (from simple letters to complex moving images) can be represented by numbers, which in turn can be represented in binary form. This means that any sort of information can be represented in digital electronic circuits. Computers *(see page 8)* rely on this fact to store numbers, words, pictures, and sounds. They use circuits called logic circuits to process and manipulate the information.

Many types of analog information must to be turned into digital form before they can be handled by digital circuits. This process is called digitization *(see illustration below)*. For example, in a microphone, a sound, which is created by waves of air pressure, is turned into a changing electric current, called an analog signal, that represents the changes in pressure. This is turned into a digital signal by an electronic circuit called an analog-to-digital converter. It repeatedly measures the analog signal, turning it into a continuous stream of binary numbers.

An image on a computer screen is made up of tiny dots called pixels. Each has a position, color and brightness, which exist as binary codes in the computer.

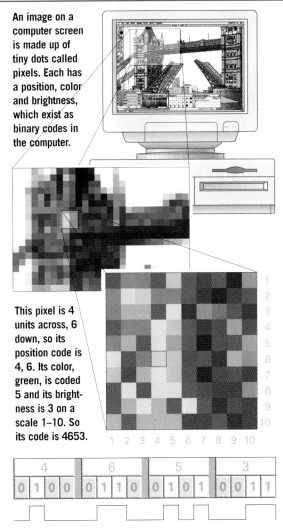

This pixel is 4 units across, 6 down, so its position code is 4, 6. Its color, green, is coded 5 and its brightness is 3 on a scale 1–10. So its code is 4653.

The pixel code is stored as a binary number, which, inside the computer, exists as electrical signals. 1 means an electrical pulse, 0 means no electrical pulse.

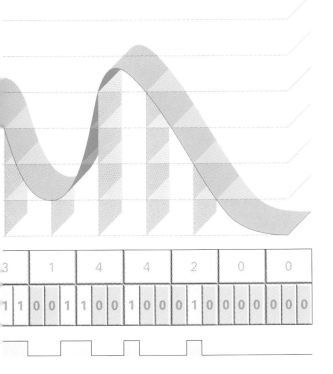

In telephone systems *(see page 12)*, the sound of your voice is digitized, normally at the telephone exchange, before it travels across the telephone network. Before it arrives at the telephone of the person you are talking to, it is turned back to an analog signal (which is needed to work the speaker) by a digital-to-analog converter. The same thing happens in a CD player, because sound is recorded in digital form on a CD *(see page 28)*.

DIGITAL PICTURES

Anything that appears on a computer's monitor is called computer graphics. These can be as simple as plain white text on a black screen, or as complicated as animated three-dimensional images. Whatever the graphics are, they are made up of small colored squares called pixels (short for picture elements) in a grid pattern.

The concentration of pixels in a picture is called resolution. High-resolution graphics can be viewed on a large screen without the pixels being visible. Graphics can have a different range of colors, too. In eight-bit graphics, each pixel is represented by eight bits, and so can be any one of 256 colors.

COMPUTERS

COMPUTERS do hundreds of different jobs, from word processing to flying aircraft. A computer can perform different tasks because it is a general-purpose electronic machine, controlled by a computer program. Change the program and the computer does a new job. A computer stores data such as numbers, words, sounds, and pictures, and processes it under direction of the program.

The first computers to work in the same way as today's were developed in the 1940s. These huge machines used thousands of thermionic valves *(see page 4)*. Computers became far smaller with the introduction of integrated circuits in the 1950s, and have continued to become more powerful.

Desktop computers used at home, school, and work are called personal computers (PCs). Other types include mainframes, used by large companies for data processing, and supercomputers, for doing complex scientific calculations extremely quickly.

The central processing unit of a PC is contained on a single large integrated circuit called a microprocessor. It has two units—one that carries out calculations and other operations, and another that receives instructions and data from memory.

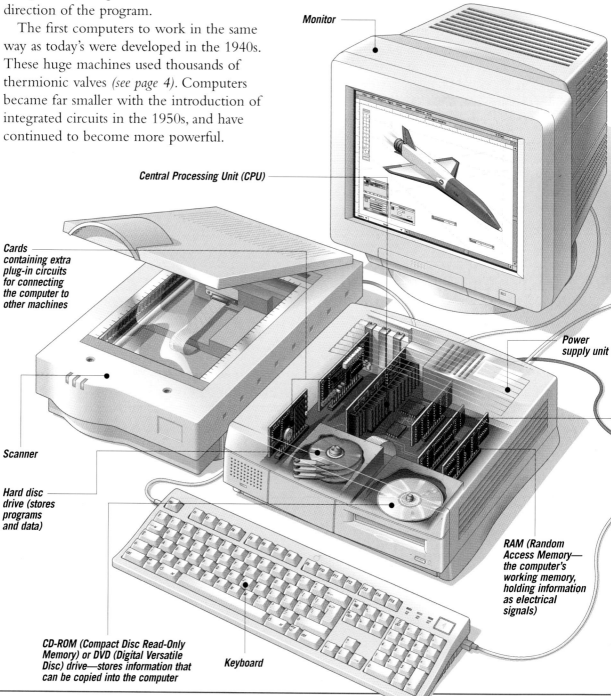

Monitor

Central Processing Unit (CPU)

Cards containing extra plug-in circuits for connecting the computer to other machines

Power supply unit

Scanner

Hard disc drive (stores programs and data)

RAM (Random Access Memory— the computer's working memory, holding information as electrical signals)

CD-ROM (Compact Disc Read-Only Memory) or DVD (Digital Versatile Disc) drive—stores information that can be copied into the computer

Keyboard

PARTS OF A PC

A computer is made up of hardware, its physical parts, and software, made up of the data and programs it stores and uses. The hardware is made up of the computer itself and peripherals, such as monitors and printers, that attach to it.

The main part of a personal computer is the central processing unit (CPU), normally simply called the processor, which can be thought of as the computer's "brain." It receives instructions from the program and carries them out. Programs and data are stored in the computer's memory. Rows of metal tracks called buses connect the processor and memory. The data bus carries the data; the address bus tells the memory where the data should come from or go to.

Robot welders, used in car manufacturing, are controlled by computers.

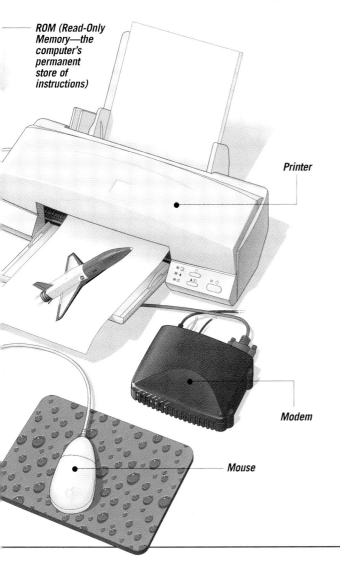

ROM (Read-Only Memory—the computer's permanent store of instructions)

Printer

Modem

Mouse

COMPUTER APPLICATIONS

There are two main types of computer software—system software and application software. System software does the computer's "housekeeping" jobs, such as controlling a printer, or writing data to disc drives. Application software makes the computer do specific jobs.

Most personal computers have application software such as a word processor (for preparing letters and reports), a database (for storing and retrieving information), a web browser (for surfing the World Wide Web) and e-mail software. Games and educational programs are also applications. Office computers may also have software for doing calculations (called spreadsheets), for processing orders, for accounts, for planning projects and for making presentations. Book and magazine designers use publishing software to design and edit pages before they are printed. Engineers and designers use computer-aided design (CAD) software to help them design new products, which they can view on-screen before making the real thing. Details of the parts can be sent to computers that control the manufacturing machines that make the parts.

In most offices, computers are linked together into networks so that they can share programs and data, which are stored on a computer called a server.

Many computers do just one specific job. Examples of these dedicated computers are games machines, in-car navigation computers, and the computers that help to fly airliners (see page 52) and fighter aircraft.

ELECTROMAGNETIC RADIATION

RADIO WAVES, microwaves, light, and X rays have different characteristics, but they are all forms of electromagnetic radiation. Together with other forms, they make up a family called the electromagnetic spectrum. These forms of radiation can also be thought of as waves moving through space, in the same way as waves move across the surface of water. They all travel at the speed of light. Forms of electromagnetic radiation can be grouped according to their wavelengths—the distance between one wave crest and the next.

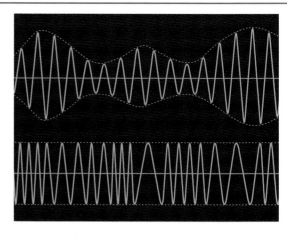

Electromagnetic waves have an amplitude and a frequency. Amplitude is the height or strength of a wave. Frequency is the number of wave crests that pass a point every second. To make a radio wave carry sound, it has to be modulated. This can be done by modulating (varying) either the strength of a wave—amplitude modulation or AM *(top)*—or the speed of a wave—frequency modulation or FM *(above)*.

In reality, the wavelength at the left-hand end of the spectrum is a million million million times the wavelength at the right-hand end.

Microwave oven

RADIO WAVES

MICROWAVES

The *Magellan* space probe used radar (RAdio Detection And Ranging) to map the surface of Venus. Instead of light, radio waves were used by the probe to build up an image of the planet's landscape.

Radio

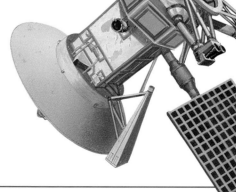

RADIO WAVES

The longest waves of the electromagnetic spectrum are radio waves. They have wavelengths ranging from more than 62 miles (100 km) down to less than 3 feet (1 m). Radio waves are produced when an electric current changes strength or direction. Radio waves are important in communications through air and space. Microwaves are high-frequency radio waves also used in communications. Some microwave frequencies can be used in cooking.

LIGHT

In the middle of the electromagnetic spectrum is a small group of waves that our eyes detect, which is called visible light. It has wavelengths of around a thousandth of a millimeter. Waves with slightly different wavelengths appear as different colors, which together make up the color spectrum. Light, and especially laser light *(see page 28),* is very important in modern communications. Where practical, it is used in place of electricity and radio waves, because it can carry far more information without problems of interference.

X RAYS AND GAMMA RAYS

To the right of ultraviolet radiation are two more forms of electromagnetic radiation— X rays and gamma rays. They both have very short wavelengths (less than a millionth of a millimeter) and extremely high frequencies (more than a million million million cycles per second). This means that X rays and gamma rays have extremely high energies, and they can pass right through some solids. This makes them useful for investigating what is inside solid objects, such as human bodies, or closed suitcases at an airport security checkpoint.

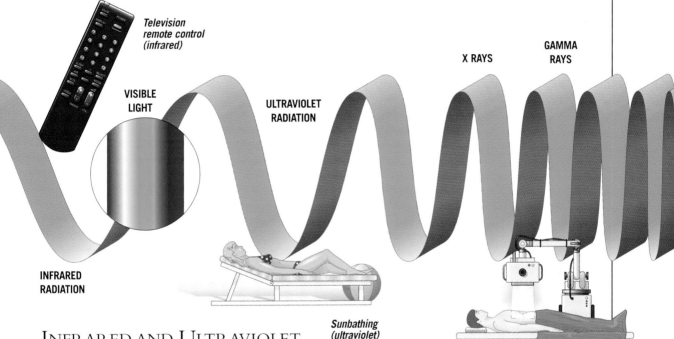

Television remote control (infrared)

VISIBLE LIGHT

ULTRAVIOLET RADIATION

X RAYS

GAMMA RAYS

INFRARED RADIATION

Sunbathing (ultraviolet)

X-ray machine

INFRARED AND ULTRAVIOLET

To the left of visible light on the spectrum is infrared (IR) radiation. This is the radiation you feel as heat from hot objects. It is one of ways in which heat energy travels. Infrared radiation is used for short-range communications, such as in television remote controls, video camera autofocus and remote locking in cars.

To the right of visible light on the spectrum is ultraviolet (UV) radiation. It carries more energy than visible light. Ultraviolet radiation from the sun is mostly absorbed by the atmosphere, but it still causes tanning of the skin and sunburn.

X rays were discovered by the German physicist Wilhelm Röntgen in 1895. They have a wide range of applications. In medicine, they are used to see the structure of bones and other organs by placing the patient between an X-ray source and a photographic film or camera. X rays and gamma rays are also used in radiotherapy for treating cancers. However, in high doses they can damage tissues. X rays are given off by high-energy, distant objects in space. X-ray telescopes can detect them.

TELECOMMUNICATIONS

TELECOMMUNICATIONS is the sending and receiving of information using electricity, radio waves, or light. The information can be sound, television pictures, or computer data (which itself can be numbers, words, sounds, and images). Forms of telecommunications include the telephone, fax, two-way radio, television and radio broadcasting, and the Internet. Most of these forms of communication require transmitting and receiving machines, and a network to link them together.

Alexander Graham Bell gave the first demonstration of the telephone in 1876, and founded the Bell Telephone Company the next year. Bell developed the telephone in his time off from working with deaf children as a speech therapist.

Morse code is a code in which letters and numbers are represented by combinations of long and short pulses of electricity, sound, or light. The code was developed in the 1830s by Samuel Morse for use on an electric telegraph

The first telecommunications device was the telegraph. Messages traveled along wires from a sending device to a receiving device as pulses of electricity, using some sort of code that both the sender and receiver understood. Practical telegraph systems were developed in the first half of the nineteenth century, and were first used for railway signaling. Early systems needed several connecting wires, but the system that eventually became standard, developed in the United States by Samuel Morse, needed just one wire. A network of telegraph lines, including undersea cables across the Atlantic, was quickly established right around the world.

In the early 1900s the telegraph was automated so that machines turned the message into code and back again. The sender could type messages on a keyboard and they would be printed out at the receiver's end. To send a telegraph message, people had to visit a telegraph office. The message arrived at another office and was delivered by hand to the recipient.

The next major step in the development of telecommunications was the invention of the telephone, which could transmit speech, allowing people far apart to talk to each other. The first telephone receiver (the part that you talk into and listen to) was patented in 1876 by Alexander Graham Bell. This device both turned the sound of the user's voice into an electrical signal, and an incoming signal into sound, which meant that the user could not talk and listen at the same time.

Early telephones had a separate mouthpiece and earpiece.

When the telephone was invented, there was no telephone network to link telephones in different places, but one soon developed. All the telephone lines in an area meet at a telephone exchange, where they can be connected to one another, or to a line to another area's exchange. The first exchange, opened in 1878 in Connecticut, had just 21 lines. Like all early exchanges, it was operated by hand. A subscriber had to tell the operator which line he or she wanted to be connected to. The automatic exchange, which allowed people to dial numbers, was invented in the United States by Almon Strowger, and started working in 1897. Meanwhile, complex telephone networks grew in large cities. It took longer for different cities and countries to be linked, and until the middle of the twentieth century, the telegraph was still used for long-distance communication.

HOW A TELEPHONE WORKS

All telephone receivers *(see illustration below)* are linked to a telephone exchange by a telephone line (1). When you lift or turn on the receiver, electronic circuits at the exchange detect it and wait for a number to be dialed. As you dial the number, the receiver sends signals to the exchange, which uses them to make a connection to the line of the person you are calling. The exchange makes the other telephone ring, and when it is answered, it connects the two lines together.

When you speak into the receiver's mouthpiece (2), the sound makes a thin metal plate called a diaphragm vibrate. This movement affects the strength of an electric current, creating an electrical copy of the sound, which is called a signal. The signal travels through the connections in the telephone network to the other receiver, where it operates a tiny speaker in the earpiece (3), recreating the sound.

The signal travels in digital form *(see page 6)* for most of its journey through the network.

A telephone exchange in 1902. In early exchanges, only callers attached to the same exchange could be automatically connected. Long-distance calls between cities and countries required three or four operators to connect them.

COMMUNICATIONS NETWORKS

TELEPHONE CALLS, fax messages, e-mails, computer data—and often radio and television signals as well—all travel from place to place through a complex, worldwide telecommunications network. All the different forms of telecommunications are turned into signals that can travel through the network. They always travel between two points in the network (for example, two telephone receivers or fax machines), and are directed through it by electronic circuits at telephone exchanges. This sort of telecommunications network is called a switched network. Radio and television networks *(see page 16),* where signals are sent to many receivers from one transmitter, are known as broadcast networks.

All the telecommunications devices (telephones, fax machines, and home computers) connected to normal telephone lines are linked by the lines to a local telephone exchange. Each line has its own unique telephone number which the exchange uses to find it. All the local exchanges in one area are linked to a main exchange, which in turn is linked to other main exchanges to form a national network. Also linked into the network are special exchanges for mobile telephones, and Internet service providers *(see opposite).* Most information (speech, fax messages, and computer data) travels to and from the local exchange in analog form and between local exchanges in digital form.

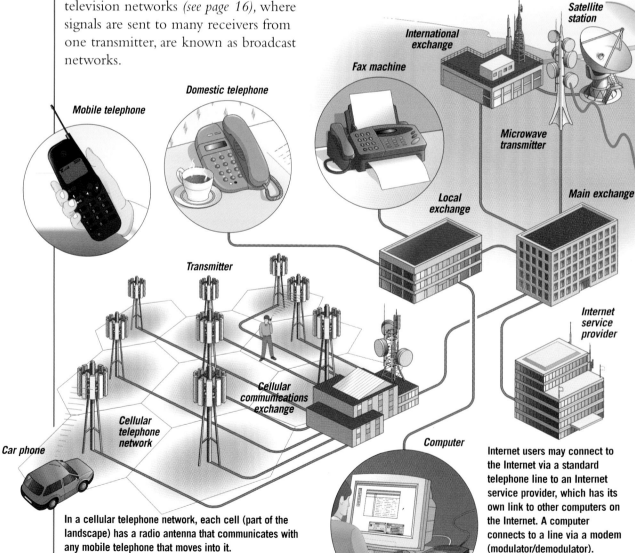

In a cellular telephone network, each cell (part of the landscape) has a radio antenna that communicates with any mobile telephone that moves into it.

Internet users may connect to the Internet via a standard telephone line to an Internet service provider, which has its own link to other computers on the Internet. A computer connects to a line via a modem (modulator/demodulator).

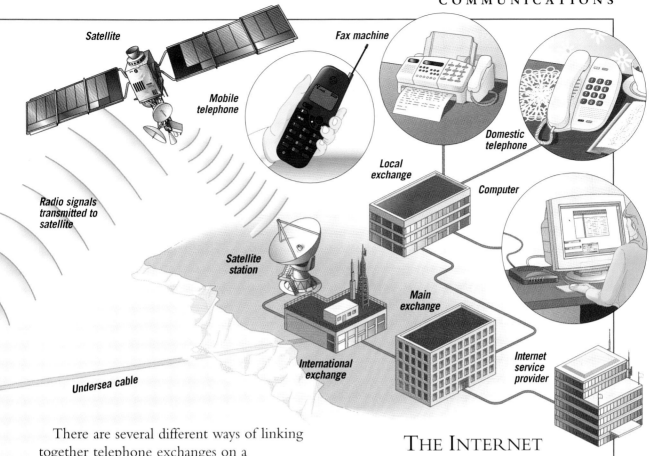

Satellite

Fax machine

Mobile telephone

Domestic telephone

Local exchange

Computer

Radio signals transmitted to satellite

Satellite station

Main exchange

Undersea cable

International exchange

Internet service provider

There are several different ways of linking together telephone exchanges on a network. Some links are underground cables, either in the form of electrical cables or optical-fiber cables, in which signals are carried by light *(see page 28)*. Some links are made with microwaves *(see below)*. International links across oceans are made via satellites in orbit around Earth, and through cables stretched across the sea bed.

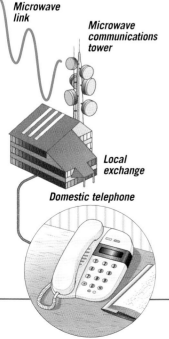

Microwave link

Microwave communications tower

Local exchange

Domestic telephone

Microwaves carry signals between hilltop transmitters and receivers, to and from communications satellites. Microwave transmitters and receivers are dish-shaped aerials. A transmitter focuses the microwaves into a narrow beam, which is aimed at a receiver that collects the waves. The microwaves are modulated (shaped) so that they can carry information.

THE INTERNET

The Internet is a vast computer network that stretches around the world, made up of hundreds of millions of computers. Data can travel from any computer on the network to any other computer. The Internet began in the 1960s, when research agencies in the United States built their own communications network. Other organizations, such as universities, gradually joined. As home computers became cheaper and more popular in the 1990s, the Internet began expanding rapidly, with anybody being able to use it via a telephone line.

Internet use falls into two main areas—e-mail and the World Wide Web. With e-mail, it is possible to send a text message (with other data files, such as photographs attached, if needed) almost instantly to any other Internet user at their e-mail address. The World Wide Web (the "Web") is a huge information-gathering system. It allows one computer connected to the Internet to ask for and copy files from another computer. The files are stored in standard form so that any computer can read them.

15

RADIO

THE WORD "radio" means communicating with radio waves, which are part of the electromagnetic spectrum *(see page 10)*. Radio has a huge range of applications. It is used in the telephone network *(see page 14)* for mobile telephones and links in the network, for broadcasting, for two-way radio communications as used by the emergency services, and for remote control of machines. "Radio" also means the media of radio, in which music and speech from radio stations are transmitted by radio waves, and are picked up by radio receivers.

The existence of radio waves was confirmed in 1888 by the German physicist Heinrich Hertz, but it was the Italian Guglielmo Marconi who, in 1896, was the first to make long-distance radio transmissions. In 1901 he transmitted Morse code *(see page 12)* across the Atlantic. Two-way radio communications using Morse code began in the early twentieth century, and radio broadcasting began in the 1920s.

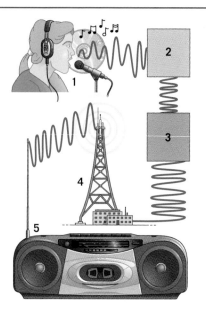

At a radio station, electrical signals from microphones, tape machines, and music decks are combined to create a signal for transmission (1). This is then modulated (2), amplified to increase its power (3), and then sent to a transmitter (4). From here radio waves spread out in all directions. They are detected by radio receivers (5).

The shaping process is called modulation *(see page 10)*. So that radio signals from different transmitters do not interfere with each other, they are sent using carrier waves with different frequencies. The whole family of radio waves is divided into sections called wavebands. Each waveband is reserved for a different form of communication. A radio receiver detects radio waves of the right frequency and demodulates them to get back the original electrical signal.

Italian radio pioneer Guglielmo Marconi with his radio equipment.

On their own, radio waves do not carry any information. To make an electrical signal, such as one representing sound, into a radio signal, the electrical signal is used to shape another signal, called the carrier wave. The shaped carrier signal is sent to a transmitter, where it creates radio waves.

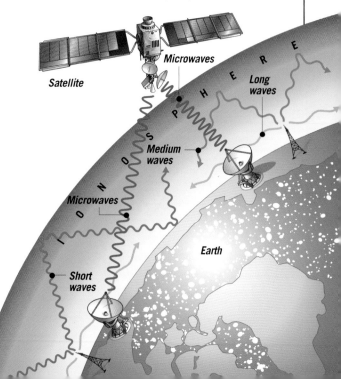

Radio waves travel through the air, bounce off a layer of the atmosphere called the ionosphere, or are relayed by satellite.

TELEVISION

THE WORD "television" means transmitting images of a moving scene (and the sound to go with them) from the scene to a different place. A simple television system needs a television camera at the scene, a way of transmitting the images *(see page 19)*, and a television receiver where the images appear. A television camera takes 25 or 30 electronic photographs (called frames) of a scene every second and creates an electric signal that represents the colors in the frames. The receiver uses this signal to display the frames in quick succession on a screen, which creates the illusion of smooth movement because our brains merge the frames together.

John Logie Baird's television equipment.

The first working television system was demonstrated in 1926 by the British pioneer John Logie Baird. It created a small, wobbly image of a dummy's face. Baird's system used a mechanical camera and receiver. These contained large spinning discs with a spiral pattern of holes in them which divided the light from the scene into narrow lines and rebuilt it into an image. Although Baird's system was used for experimental broadcasts, it was made redundant in the 1930s by systems that used fully electronic cameras. These were based on a device called iconoscope, developed in the United States by Vladimir Zworykin. The first broadcasting service started in Britain in 1936, with one or two hours of programs being shown each day.

HOW A TV SET WORKS

A television receiver (or set) builds each frame of the moving television picture line by line, using the electrical signal originally created by the camera to control the color of the dots along the lines. In most television receivers, the picture is created by a cathode-ray tube.

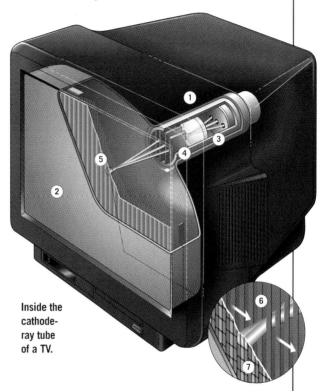

Inside the cathode-ray tube of a TV.

The cathode-ray tube in a television receiver has a narrow neck (1) and a flat base that forms the screen (2). The air is pumped out to create a vacuum. At the back of the tube are three guns (3) that fire beams of electrons (for red, green, and blue light) at the screen. Electromagnets (4) make the beams scan quickly across the screen line by line, while the picture signal controls their strength. Where the beams hit a special coating on the inside of the screen, it gives off light (5). Just behind the TV screen is a plate with holes in it called a shadow mask (6). It ensures that the beams hit the screen only behind filters of their own color (7). Filters make the light produced by the three beams appear red, blue, or green. These combine to form the picture colors.

Television programs such as news, talk shows, and games shows are made in a large room at the television station called a studio (1). Each program has its own backgrounds and furniture called a set. Cameras (2) and microphones (3) send signals to the control room (4). Lighting comes from powerful lamps (5).

BROADCASTING

THERE ARE thousands of different television channels around the world, broadcasting entertainment, news, information, and sports. Television programs are created at television stations. Each station normally broadcasts several separate channels. Some programs, such as news and sports, are broadcast live, which means the viewers see action as it happens. Most programs are recorded on videotape and broadcast at a later date. Some programs are a combination of live and recorded action.

A television camera electronically divides an image of the scene it is pointing at into hundreds of narrow horizontal lines, each made up of hundreds of small dots of color. It creates an electrical signal that represents the colors of all the dots. It repeats this process 25 or 30 times a second to create a continuous picture signal.

Pictures from the cameras in a television studio, and from cameras at outside broadcasts, such as sporting events, are fed to a control room, where they appear on screens. Here, live pictures from cameras, pictures from videotape (such as short news reports), and computer graphics are mixed to create the signal for the pictures that will be broadcast. Sound from studio microphones or audio tape is also added.

There are several ways of broadcasting signals. In each case, the signal is modulated *(see page 10)* before it is sent, with different channels using different carrier signals. The receiver tunes in to the signal from the channel the viewer wants to watch. Many signals now travel in digital *(see page 6)* rather than analog form. This allows many more channels to be broadcast, and eliminates the interference that often makes pictures sent using analog signals fuzzy.

In terrestrial television, the signal goes to a transmitter where it is turned into a radio signal that is spread out in all directions. The signal can be detected by an antenna of any receiver within range of the transmitter. In cable television, the signal travels from a cable television station through a network of underground cables that link directly to receivers connected to the network. In satellite television, the signal is beamed by microwaves to a satellite high above the earth. The satellite detects the signal with its own antenna and retransmits it so that it can be picked up by receivers on the earth's surface. In webcasting, television and video pictures are transmitted over the Internet *(see page 15)*. The pictures are first converted into a digital video format and then made available on a website.

In closed-circuit television (CCTV), signals are not broadcast at all. Instead, they go directly from the camera to a receiver. CCTV is used for security systems, with the pictures being recorded as well as viewed.

Terrestrial television signals are broadcast from transmitters (1) at the top of tall masts, often on hilltops, and detected by antennae (2) placed high up on roofs. This gives the signals a clear route from transmitter to antennae. But in mountainous areas the signals are often blocked by hills. This is not a problem with satellite television, where the signals come down from a satellite high in the sky to small dishes (3) aimed accurately at the satellite.

Interactive television is television in which the viewer can send information back to the television station, normally via a telephone line. The combination of digital television and a telephone line also allows viewers to access the Internet *(see page 15)*.

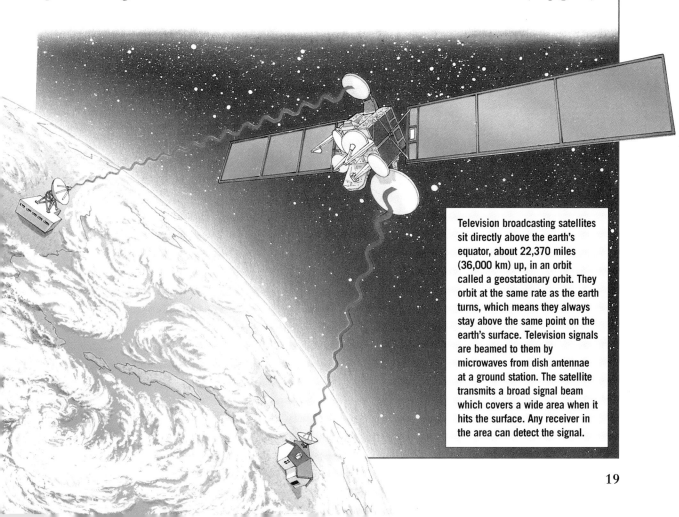

Television broadcasting satellites sit directly above the earth's equator, about 22,370 miles (36,000 km) up, in an orbit called a geostationary orbit. They orbit at the same rate as the earth turns, which means they always stay above the same point on the earth's surface. Television signals are beamed to them by microwaves from dish antennae at a ground station. The satellite transmits a broad signal beam which covers a wide area when it hits the surface. Any receiver in the area can detect the signal.

PRINTING

PRINTING is the process of making many copies of a document or a picture. Printing is normally done on paper, but it can also be done on fabrics and sheets of plastic or metal. Books such as this one are printed on a machine called a printing press. The text and pictures start as patterns on a plate. In the press, the plate is inked so that these areas become ink-covered, and are pressed onto the paper via a rubber-covered drum. A fast printing press can make several prints a second because each print is made by one simple operation.

One of the first methods of printing was wood-block printing, where the images to be printed were carved in reverse into wooden blocks. The blocks were then inked and pressed onto paper to make a print. Ink from the raised areas was transferred on to the paper. Simple block printing is still used for hand-printed textiles.

Two of the most important inventions in printing were moveable metal type (which allowed words and paragraphs to be built up from individual metal blocks with letters on them) and the printing press. In Europe, these were both developed in the fifteenth century by the German printing pioneer Johannes Gutenberg. They allowed books to be printed in large quantities, whereas before each book had to be hand-copied.

On a printed color page such as this one, the text is normally solid black ink, while the pictures are made up of tiny dots of colored—and black—ink.

In an early printing press a screw was turned to press the paper firmly down onto inked type.

Most color printing is done with just four colors of ink: cyan, magenta, yellow, and black. By printing dots in varying sizes, the first three colors combine to create almost any other color *(right)*. In practice, all three mix to create brown, so black is used to darken some areas.

Cyan only

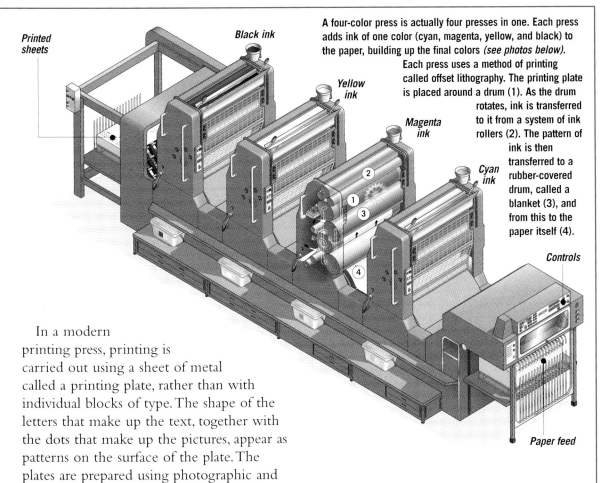

Printed sheets

Black ink

Yellow ink

Magenta ink

Cyan ink

A four-color press is actually four presses in one. Each press adds ink of one color (cyan, magenta, yellow, and black) to the paper, building up the final colors *(see photos below).* Each press uses a method of printing called offset lithography. The printing plate is placed around a drum (1). As the drum rotates, ink is transferred to it from a system of ink rollers (2). The pattern of ink is then transferred to a rubber-covered drum, called a blanket (3), and from this to the paper itself (4).

Controls

Paper feed

In a modern printing press, printing is carried out using a sheet of metal called a printing plate, rather than with individual blocks of type. The shape of the letters that make up the text, together with the dots that make up the pictures, appear as patterns on the surface of the plate. The plates are prepared using photographic and chemical processes.

Type and pictures for a book, magazine, or pamphlets are nowadays usually designed and laid out on a computer using desktop publishing software. The files from the computer may then be sent to the printer, which uses them to make four printing plates, one for each color of ink on the printing press.

For most publications, the paper needs to be printed on both sides. Some presses can do this but on others the paper has to be sent through the press twice. Several pages of the final book or magazine are normally printed on each sheet of paper. The sheets then go for print finishing, where machines fold, collate (sort), staple or sew, and trim the sheets to create the finished product.

Cyan and magenta

Cyan, magenta, and yellow

Cyan, magenta, yellow, and black

21

CAMERAS AND PHOTOGRAPHY

A CAMERA is a device that records an image of a scene, either on photographic film or electronically as a digital photograph. Its main features are a light-proof body, a lens, and a shutter. The lens gathers rays of light from the scene that the camera is pointed at and bends them so that all the rays from one point on the scene are focused to meet at the same place at the back of the camera. In this way it makes a small copy of the scene called an image. The shutter opens to allow light from the lens to reach the film or light sensors. Photographic film must be exposed to just the right amount of light in order to create a clear image on the film. The exposure is controlled by adjusting how long the shutter opens for (called the shutter speed) and the size of an opening behind the lens, called the aperture.

In 1888 American inventor George Eastman introduced the first Kodak box camera. It helped to make photography a popular hobby because the film could be sent away for developing.

The forerunner of the camera was the camera obscura, used by artists, which made images with a lens but could not record them. The earliest surviving photograph was taken by Frenchman Joseph Niépce in 1827. It was recorded on a metal plate coated with chemicals that changed very slowly where the image was light but not where it was dark. Photographic processes were soon improved by Frenchman Louis Daguerre and Englishman William Fox Talbot. Talbot developed the negative-positive process, where the image is recorded as a negative in the camera, and is used to print positive photographs.

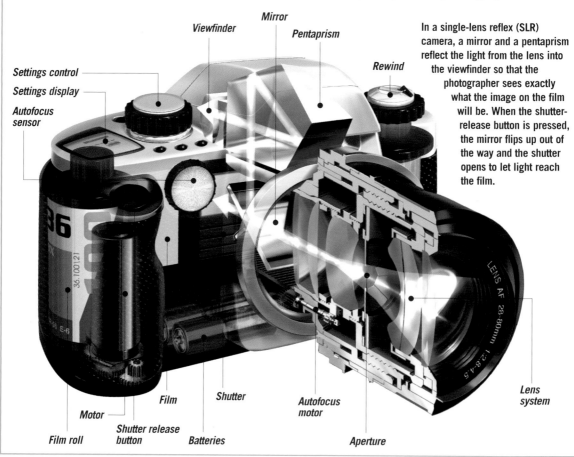

In a single-lens reflex (SLR) camera, a mirror and a pentaprism reflect the light from the lens into the viewfinder so that the photographer sees exactly what the image on the film will be. When the shutter-release button is pressed, the mirror flips up out of the way and the shutter opens to let light reach the film.

Mirror

Viewfinder

Pentaprism

Rewind

Settings control

Settings display

Autofocus sensor

Film

Motor

Shutter

Autofocus motor

Lens system

Film roll

Shutter release button

Batteries

Aperture

RECORDING AN IMAGE

Photographic film consists of a plastic strip coated on one side with a layer of light-sensitive chemicals. When light from a scene is focused onto the film in a camera, the chemicals in the bright areas of the image begin to change. The brighter the light, the greater the change. The chemicals remain unchanged in the dark areas. At this stage, the image is simply a pattern of chemicals. It only becomes visible when the film is processed. Color film contains three layers of chemicals, one to record each of the primary colors of light, which are red, green, and blue.

The Imacon high-speed research camera takes photographs just one billionth of a second apart. It can reveal what happens when a bullet hits its target.

DIGITAL PHOTOGRAPHY

A digital camera is a camera in which photographs are stored electronically in digital form rather than on traditional film. The lens focuses light onto a special microchip called a charge-coupled device (CCD). This divides the image into pixels *(see page 6),* measures the brightness and color of each one, and digitizes the readings. The digitized image is stored in memory chips or on a disc. The photographs are transferred to a computer, where they can be viewed on screen, edited, added to documents, used to make greetings cards, or attached to e-mails.

MOVIE CAMERAS

American inventor Thomas Edison built his kinetoscope *(right)* in the late 1891 to show films shot by his kinetograph, which was one of the first movie cameras. The viewer watched the movie, which was on a continuous loop of film, through a slot in the top of the kinetoscope.

A MOVIE FILM is made up of thousands of photographs called frames on a long roll of film. The frames are taken in quick succession by a movie camera (or cine-camera). A revolving shutter opens to let light hit the film, creating the image for a frame. Then it closes and the film is moved into position for the next frame. This sequence is repeated again and again to photograph 24 frames every second.

A movie projector *(below)* does the reverse of a camera. It shines a bright light through the film and focuses the rays onto a screen, creating an enlarged image. It shows the frames in quick succession, which creates the illusion of movement.

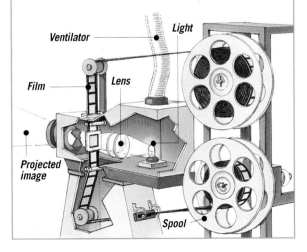

Ventilator

Light

Film

Lens

Projected image

Spool

MICROSCOPES

A MICROSCOPE is an instrument that magnifies very small objects, allowing the viewer to see detail in the object that is invisible to the naked eye. Microscopes are used mostly, but not only, in biology and medical research.

There are two main types of microscope—optical microscopes and electron microscopes. In an optical microscope, the image of the object is created by light. The simplest optical microscope is a magnifying glass, which contains a single lens. The lens gathers and bends light coming from the object, making the object look larger than it really is. Compound microscopes have more than one lens. A standard compound microscope has two groups of lenses. The first group, called the objective, gathers light from the object and focuses it to create a magnified image of the object. The second group, called the eyepiece, magnifies this image.

French microbiologist Louis Pasteur (above) studies bacteria under a microscope.

The first compound microscope was probably built by Dutch spectacle-maker Zacharias Janssen in about 1590. Early microscopes had poor-quality lenses and gave blurred images. In the 1670s another Dutchman, Anton van Leeuwenhoek, began making simple, single-lens microscopes. He was the first person to see microorganisms such as bacteria and amoebas.

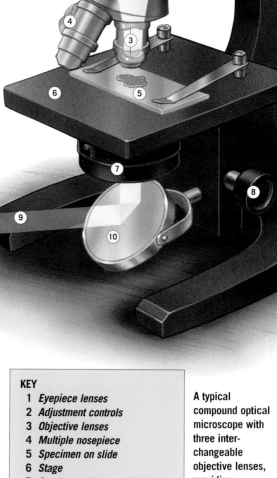

KEY
1 *Eyepiece lenses*
2 *Adjustment controls*
3 *Objective lenses*
4 *Multiple nosepiece*
5 *Specimen on slide*
6 *Stage*
7 *Condenser (focuses light beam)*
8 *Condenser control*
9 *Light beam*
10 *Mirror*

A typical compound optical microscope with three inter-changeable objective lenses, providing magnifications from about 50 times to about 200 times.

ELECTRON MICROSCOPES

Optical microscopes can only magnify objects up to 2,000 times. Greater magnifications do not reveal any more detail. Electron microscopes can magnify objects more than a million times. In an electron microscope, a beam of tiny particles called electrons does the same job as light in an optical microscope. It is fired at the object and then focused by electromagnetic "lenses" on to a screen that emits light where the electrons hit it.

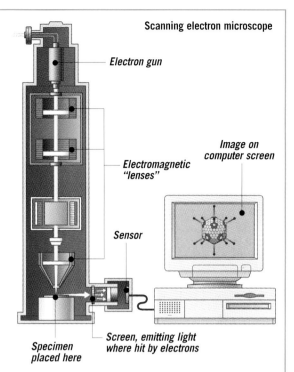

Scanning electron microscope

Electron gun

Electromagnetic "lenses"

Image on computer screen

Sensor

Specimen placed here

Screen, emitting light where hit by electrons

This SEM image of the head of a fruit fly, enlarged about 135 times, has been coloured so that its features can be seen clearly.

There are two main types of electron microscope. In a transmitting electron microscope (TEM), the beam of electrons is fired through an extremely thin slice of the specimen under investigation. In a scanning electron microscope (SEM), a very narrow beam of electrons is fired at the surface of the specimen. The beam scans across the surface of the specimen and a sensor detects the electrons bouncing off. In this way, a three-dimensional image of the specimen is gradually built up.

The images created by electron microscopes are called electron photomicrographs. An example of one is shown here *(left)*. They may be viewed on television screens using video cameras, or digitized and viewed on computer screens.

The first electron microscope, which could magnify objects up to 400 times, was built in 1932 by German engineers Ernst Ruska and Max Knoll. The newest type of electron microscope is the scanning tunnelling electron microscope (STM). It can magnify up to 100 million times, which is enough to see individual atoms.

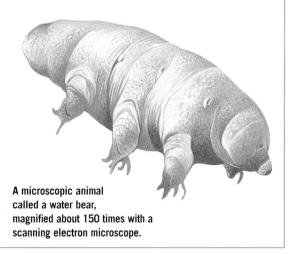

A microscopic animal called a water bear, magnified about 150 times with a scanning electron microscope.

TELESCOPES

A TELESCOPE is an instrument that makes distant objects appear closer, allowing the viewer to see details that are not visible with the naked eye. Terrestrial telescopes are used for spotting wildlife (binoculars are made up of two telescopes, one for each eye), on gun sights, and in periscopes. Astronomical telescopes are used to study objects in space. Terrestrial telescopes and most astronomical telescopes are optical telescopes, which collect light coming from distant objects and use it to produce images of the objects.

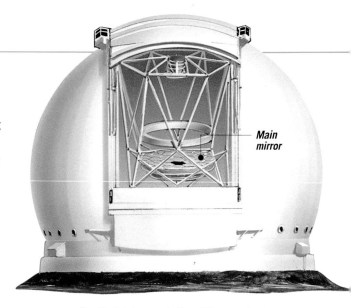

The Keck telescope in Hawaii has a main mirror 32 feet (10 m) across. It is housed in a special building called an observatory.

Italian scientist Galileo used the first astronomical telescope in 1609, with which he discovered moons around Jupiter.

The larger the lens of a refracting telescope or the mirror of a reflecting telescope, the brighter the image of the object observed, and the fainter the objects that can be seen with the telescope. The image is viewed with an eyepiece lens, which works like a magnifying glass to make it appear much larger.

A radio telescope *(below)* can be turned to collect rays from any part of the sky.

There are two main types of optical telescope—refracting telescopes and reflecting telescopes. In a refracting telescope, a convex (bulging) lens collects light from the distant object and focuses it to form an image of the object. This image is very small, but is much larger than the image formed in the human eye. In a reflecting telescope, a concave (dish-shaped) mirror collects the light from the object and focuses it to form the image. Larger telescopes are nearly always reflecting telescopes because large mirrors are easier to manufacture than large lenses.

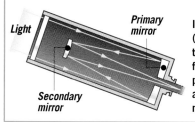

In a reflecting (Cassegrain-type) telescope, light is focused by a large primary mirror and a small secondary mirror.

RADIO TELESCOPES

Objects in space, such as stars and galaxies, do not just give off light. They also give off radiation from other parts of the electro-magnetic spectrum *(see page 10),* such as infrared radiation, radio waves, X rays, and ultraviolet radiation. These can show up objects that are otherwise invisible. They cannot be seen with ordinary optical telescopes, so special telescopes are needed.

Radio telescopes have a huge dish that acts as a reflector, collecting radio waves and focusing them onto a detector. Radio astronomy has allowed the discovery of new celestial objects, such as pulsars.

SPACE TELESCOPES

The earth's atmosphere stops many types of radiation from reaching the surface. To study these sorts of radiation, space telescopes must be launched into Earth orbit. They need special mirrors to reflect and focus the radiation, and electronic detectors to record the images formed, which are radioed back to Earth. Optical telescopes also benefit from being in orbit because the atmosphere distorts light rays as they pass through it. The Hubble space telescope, launched by space shuttle in 1990, is the most complex space telescope so far. It can detect visible light, infrared and ultraviolet rays.

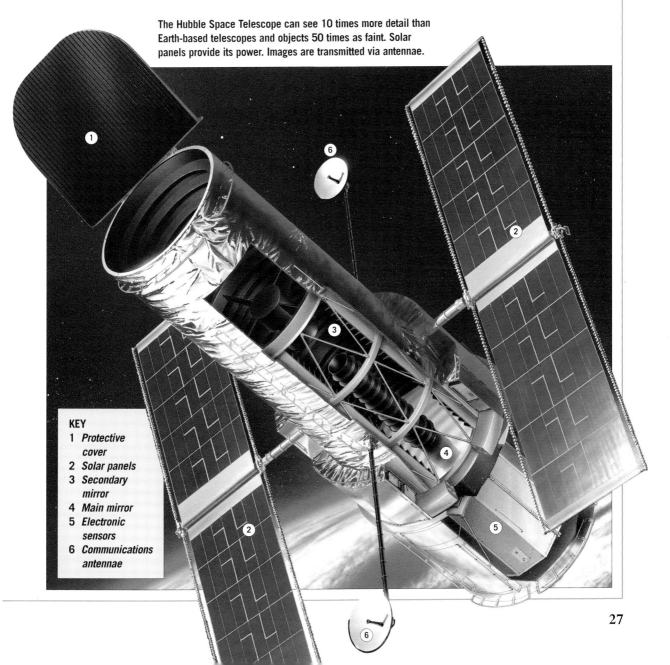

The Hubble Space Telescope can see 10 times more detail than Earth-based telescopes and objects 50 times as faint. Solar panels provide its power. Images are transmitted via antennae.

KEY
1 Protective cover
2 Solar panels
3 Secondary mirror
4 Main mirror
5 Electronic sensors
6 Communications antennae

27

LASERS

A LASER is a device that creates an intense beam of light called a laser beam. A laser beam is monochromatic: It is made up of light of just one color of the spectrum. This means that all the light waves in it have the same wavelength *(see page 10)*. Just as importantly, all the waves are "in phase," which means that as they leave the laser, their crests and troughs all line up with each other.

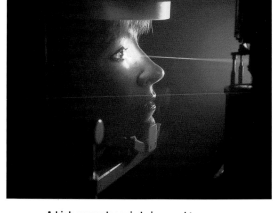

A high-power laser is being used to perform eye surgery *(above)*. If the retina, the part of the eye that contains light-sensitive cells, becomes detached, a laser beam can stick it back in place.

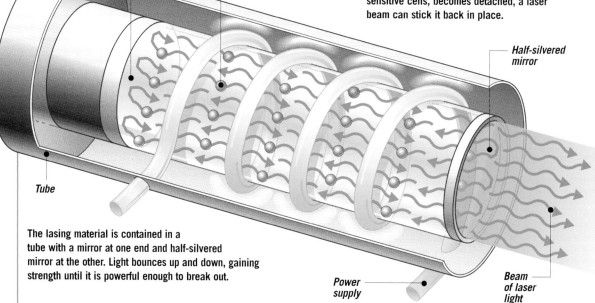

Mirror

Excited atom

Half-silvered mirror

Tube

Power supply

Beam of laser light

The lasing material is contained in a tube with a mirror at one end and half-silvered mirror at the other. Light bounces up and down, gaining strength until it is powerful enough to break out.

The word *laser* is short for Light Amplification by Stimulated Emission of Radiation. Inside the laser is lasing material, which can be a solid, a liquid, or a gas. The atoms of the material are excited or "stimulated" by giving them energy, either in the form of light or electricity. This makes them emit light (a type of radiation), which in turn makes other atoms emit light of the same wavelength. This process creates an intense laser beam. The wavelength, and so the color, of a laser beam depends on the lasing material. Some lasers produce ultraviolet or infrared radiation rather than visible light. The first working laser was built by American physicist Theodore Maiman in 1960.

USES FOR LASERS

The most common uses of lasers are playing compact discs *(see page 29)* and reading bar codes. These lasers are normally red lasers that use semiconductor lasing materials. They are low-power lasers, but they are still dangerous to look at directly. Low-power lasers are also used in communications, where they send signals along optical-fiber cables, in laser printers, in surveying, and for light shows. High-power lasers can be focused to create intense heat in materials. They are used in manufacturing for accurate cutting and in medicine for delicate surgery *(top)*.

RECORDING

TO RECORD SOUND, the pattern of vibrations in the air must be turned into a form that can be stored. The gramophone was the first sound-recording device. To record, the sound was made to vibrate a needle, which cut a wavy groove in a foil surface. To play back, the needle moved along the groove, making a diaphragm vibrate to reproduce the sound. In the electric gramophone, introduced in the 1920s, the vibrating needle created an electrical signal, which was amplified to drive a loudspeaker.

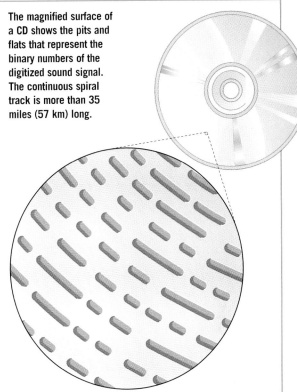

The magnified surface of a CD shows the pits and flats that represent the binary numbers of the digitized sound signal. The continuous spiral track is more than 35 miles (57 km) long.

The first type of gramophone was the phonograph, invented in 1877 by the American inventor Thomas Edison.

Most sound recording is now done digitally. A microphone turns the sound into an analog electrical signal, which is then digitized *(see page 6)* more than 44,000 times a second to create a long string of binary numbers. The binary numbers can be stored in a computer's memory or disc drives, or on a compact disc (CD). On a CD, the binary digits 0 and 1 are represented by flat areas or shallow pits in the surface. In a CD player, these are detected by a laser as the disc spins and reflected to a light-sensitive device *(below)*. Electronics rebuild the original electric signal, which is amplified and sent to speakers. Computer CD-ROMs and DVDs work in the same way.

Tape recording was developed in the 1940s. To record onto tape, the electrical signal from a microphone is sent to an electromagnet, which creates a pattern in the tiny magnetic particles that coat the tape. This pattern re-creates the signal as the tape plays, and the signal is amplified before going to a speaker.

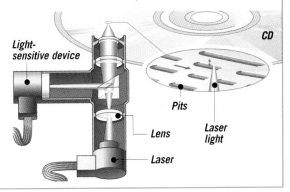

Light-sensitive device

CD

Pits

Lens

Laser light

Laser

STEAM ENGINES

AN ENGINE is a machine that converts the energy stored in fuel into energy for operating other machines. In a steam engine, burning fuel heats water in a boiler, turning it to steam, which builds up in the boiler. The pressurized steam is used to operate the moving parts of the engine. In the first century A.D., the Greek inventor Hero built a device that was turned by jets of steam, but it was a curiosity rather than a useful machine.

The first steam-powered machine was built in 1698 by English engineer Thomas Savery. It was designed to pump water from flooded mines, but was never actually used. In Savery's engine, steam from the boiler filled a large cylinder. Then cold water was poured over the outside of the cylinder, which cooled it, making the steam condense (turn back to liquid water). This created a vacuum in the cylinder, which sucked in water from the mine through a pipe. More steam was fed to the cylinder to push the water up an outlet pipe.

Thomas Savery called his steam engine the miner's friend. It pumped water from the pipe at the bottom into the pipe at the top via the two large cylinders.

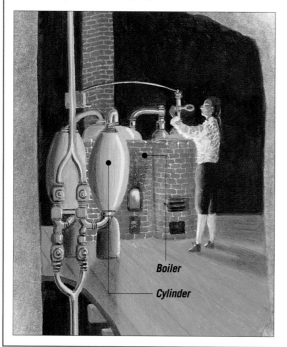

Boiler

Cylinder

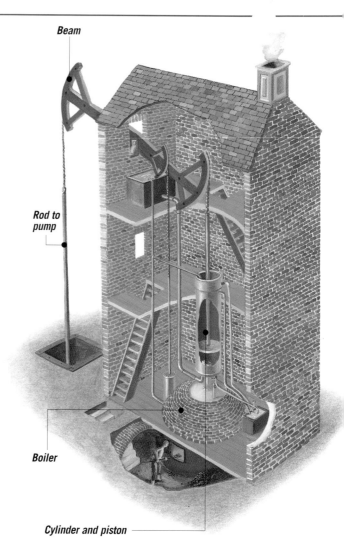

Beam

Rod to pump

Boiler

Cylinder and piston

In Thomas Newcomen's atmospheric steam engine, movement of the piston was transferred to the pump by a rocking beam.

In 1712 another English engineer, Thomas Newcomen, also completed a steam engine for pumping mine water. In Newcomen's engine, steam from the boiler went along pipes to a cylinder, where its pressure pushed a piston upward. Then cold water was sprayed into the cylinder, which made the steam condense. This reduced the pressure in the cylinder, and the pressure of the air in the atmosphere outside pushed the piston back down. This is why Newcomen's engine is often called an atmospheric engine. Although it used a huge amount of coal, it was very successful, especially at coal mines, where there was an endless supply of coal.

WATT'S IMPROVEMENTS

Steam engine design was greatly improved in the 1770s by Scottish engineer James Watt. He realized that Newcomen's engine was very inefficient because the cylinder was heated and cooled on every cycle. So Watt built his own engine, which became popular for powering industrial machinery, such as spinning and weaving machines.

Steam engines are still used today in power stations in the form of the steam turbine, where high-pressure steam makes a fan-like turbine spin at high speed.

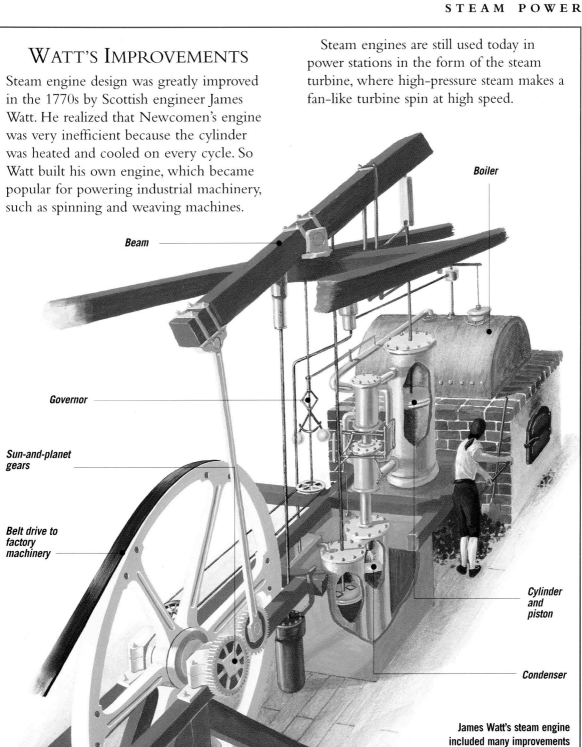

Beam

Boiler

Governor

Sun-and-planet gears

Belt drive to factory machinery

Cylinder and piston

Condenser

James Watt's steam engine included many improvements over Thomas Newcomen's. It had a separate cylinder where the steam was condensed, allowing the main cylinder to remain hot all the time. The piston was double-acting, which means it was moved both up and down by steam. This was achieved by feeding steam to one side of the piston then the other. An automatic governor controlled the flow of steam to the cylinder, and so regulated its speed. Sun-and-planet gears converted the up-and-down movement of the cylinder into a turning movement.

STEAM TRAINS

A TRAIN is a vehicle that runs on guide rails called a railway. Miners have used simple wooden or iron railways called wagon-ways for hundreds of years to move rock, coal, and ore in trucks. The trucks were pulled and pushed by animals or the miners themselves. The first locomotive powered by a steam engine *(see page 30)* was built in 1804 by English engineer Richard Trevithick, to haul trucks at an ironworks. The first passenger railway was the Stockton and Darlington Railway in England, which opened in 1828.

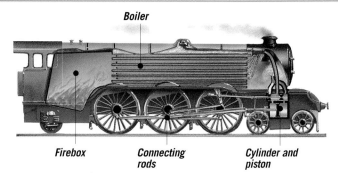

Boiler

Firebox   Connecting rods   Cylinder and piston

HOW A STEAM LOCOMOTIVE WORKS

A steam locomotive is simply a steam engine on wheels. Fuel burns in the firebox, creating hot gases that pass along tubes inside the boiler. The heat from the tubes boils the water, creating steam. As more steam collects at the top of the boiler, its pressure builds up, and it escapes along pipes to the cylinders, where, controlled by valves, it pushes the pistons one way then the other (this is called double action). The sliding motion of the pistons moves the large driving wheels around via a system of linked connecting rods.

Trevithick's locomotive could pull up to 11 tons (10 tonnes) of iron.

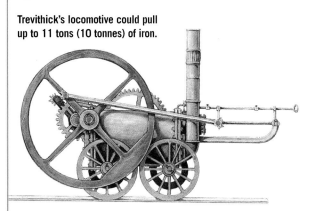

The *Rocket* *(below)*, built in England by George Stephenson, hauled trains on the Stockton and Darlington Railway.

A typical late–19th-century American locomotive *(below)*, with a "cowcatcher" at the front.

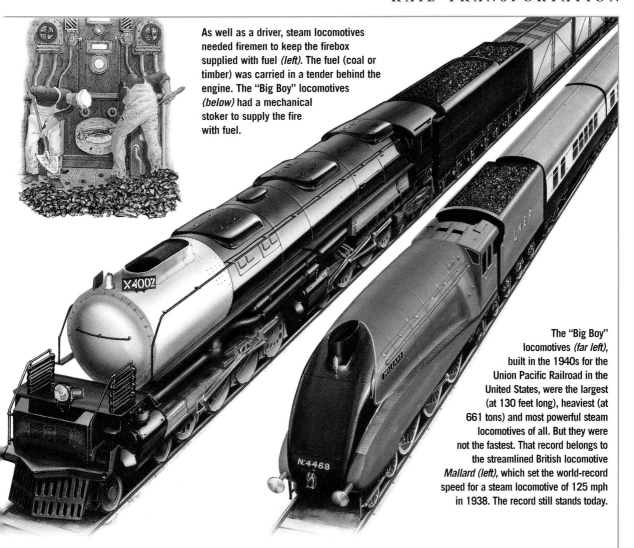

As well as a driver, steam locomotives needed firemen to keep the firebox supplied with fuel *(left)*. The fuel (coal or timber) was carried in a tender behind the engine. The "Big Boy" locomotives *(below)* had a mechanical stoker to supply the fire with fuel.

The "Big Boy" locomotives *(far left)*, built in the 1940s for the Union Pacific Railroad in the United States, were the largest (at 130 feet long), heaviest (at 661 tons) and most powerful steam locomotives of all. But they were not the fastest. That record belongs to the streamlined British locomotive *Mallard (left)*, which set the world-record speed for a steam locomotive of 125 mph in 1938. The record still stands today.

SPREAD OF THE RAILWAYS

Extensive railway networks were developed during the second half of the nineteenth century, especially in the United States, Canada, Europe, and Russia. Improvements in tracks, including the introduction of steel rails in the 1860s, allowed for heavier locomotives, with increased power and speed. Carriage design also improved, and dining cars and sleeping cars were introduced by George Pullman in the United States. Railway networks relied on other engineering improvements. Long-span steel bridges carried trains over wide rivers, and rock tunnels took them under mountain ranges such as the Alps. From the 1850s the electric telegraph *(see page 12)* allowed communications between stations so that signaling staff could keep track of where the trains were.

By the 1930s powerful, streamlined steam locomotives could haul passenger trains at high speeds. But steam locomotives are very inefficient. Only about 5 percent of the energy in the fuel gets to the wheels, and time is needed to start the fire and get the water boiling. In the 1950s and 1960s, steam locomotives disappeared from most railways and were replaced by electric-powered and diesel-powered locomotives. However, steam engines are still used in some countries, such as India and China.

Electric locomotives ran as early as 1879 in Germany. In 1890 they began pulling trains on underground railways in London, and in 1903 on mainline railways in Europe. Diesel locomotives started operating in the United States in the 1930s.

MODERN TRAINS

THERE ARE three types of modern locomotive—electric, diesel-electric, and diesel. On an electric locomotive, the wheels are moved by electric motors (normally one for each pair of wheels). The electricity usually comes from overhead cables, but sometimes from an electrified third rail. On a diesel-electric locomotive, the wheels are also driven by electric motors, but the electricity comes from a generator driven by a powerful diesel engine. On a diesel locomotive, a diesel engine drives the wheels via a mechanical transmission. Diesel locomotives are normally used only for shunting and on low-speed local trains. The fastest express trains, such as the French *Train à Grande Vitesse* (TGV), are normally electrically powered, with a locomotive at each end.

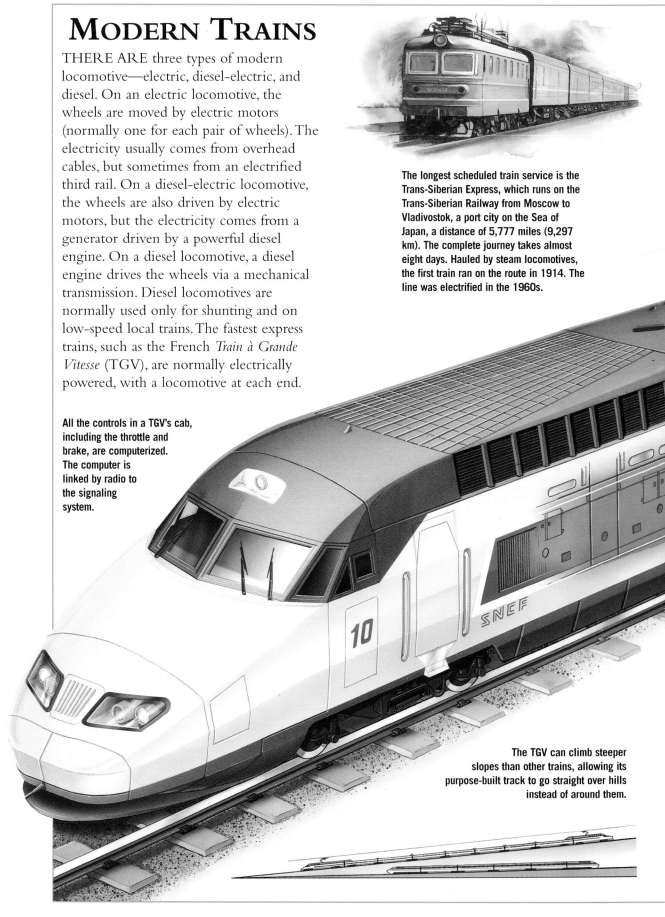

The longest scheduled train service is the Trans-Siberian Express, which runs on the Trans-Siberian Railway from Moscow to Vladivostok, a port city on the Sea of Japan, a distance of 5,777 miles (9,297 km). The complete journey takes almost eight days. Hauled by steam locomotives, the first train ran on the route in 1914. The line was electrified in the 1960s.

All the controls in a TGV's cab, including the throttle and brake, are computerized. The computer is linked by radio to the signaling system.

The TGV can climb steeper slopes than other trains, allowing its purpose-built track to go straight over hills instead of around them.

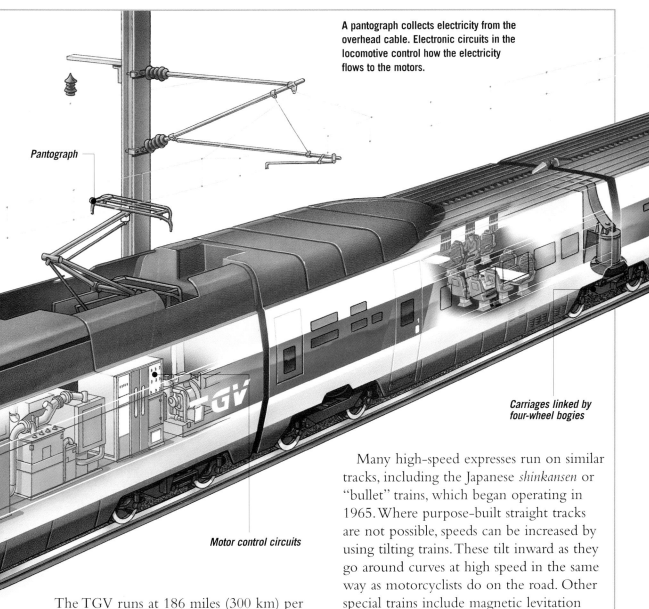

A pantograph collects electricity from the overhead cable. Electronic circuits in the locomotive control how the electricity flows to the motors.

Pantograph

Carriages linked by four-wheel bogies

Motor control circuits

The TGV runs at 186 miles (300 km) per hour—half as fast again as most express trains—and holds the world-record speed of 320 miles (515 km) per hour. It runs on a purpose-built track, which has few bends, and uses computerized signaling.

Many high-speed expresses run on similar tracks, including the Japanese *shinkansen* or "bullet" trains, which began operating in 1965. Where purpose-built straight tracks are not possible, speeds can be increased by using tilting trains. These tilt inward as they go around curves at high speed in the same way as motorcyclists do on the road. Other special trains include magnetic levitation (maglev) trains, which are both supported above their tracks and propelled by magnets. Maglev trains can reach very high speeds because there is no friction between the train and the track.

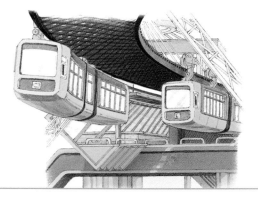

Specialized trains are often used in city centers. In Wuppertal, Germany *(left)*, trains are suspended in the air from a monorail (single rail) track. Underground trains *(right)* always use electricity because this does not create fumes. They have good acceleration in order to move quickly between closely spaced stations.

SAILING SHIPS

PEOPLE made their first journeys across water tens of thousands of years ago. Their first craft must have been logs, used as buoyancy aids. Later, they tied logs together to make rafts, or hollowed them out to make canoes. Where there were no big trees, they made boats from locally available materials, such as reeds or animal skins. Their boats allowed them to travel on rivers and lakes, searching for better fishing, or visiting hunting grounds.

These early craft were propelled by simple paddles, or poles pushed into the river bed. The first sailing boats we know about were built in ancient Egypt in about 3500 B.C. Some were built from reeds bundled together, others from wood. They had a single mast with a square sail, which was used in addition to oars when the wind was blowing in a favorable direction. The crew steered with long oars hanging over the stern (rear).

The ancient Greeks and Romans used sturdy, seaworthy cargo boats and sleek fighting boats called galleys, both with a square sail. In battle, the galleys were propelled with oars and attacked enemy ships with a ram on their bows.

About 1,000 years ago, the Vikings, who lived in northern Europe, started to explore new lands. Their ships were called knorrs (above). Each had a hull (body of vessel) made of overlapping or "clinkered" planks.

Chinese boats called junks (above) had sails stiffened by thick bamboo poles, and a sternpost rudder for steering. Until the 15th century they were the world's biggest and best boats.

A highly decorated royal boat from ancient Egypt. The two steering oars at the stern are supported by strong poles.

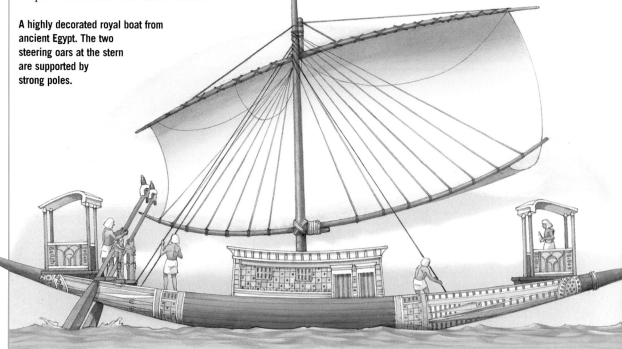

By the 16th century, small, sturdy ships such as carracks *(left)* and galleons were capable of long ocean crossings. With the aid of compasses to stop them accidentally sailing in circles, sailors set out from European ports to explore the world and to try to find new sea routes to the Spice Islands of Asia.

Among these explorers was the Portuguese navigator Ferdinand Magellan, who left Spain in 1519 with five ships to sail to Asia around the southern tip of newly discovered America. Magellan himself was killed in the Philippines, two years into the voyage. Only one of the ships, the *Vittoria,* under the captaincy of Sebastian del Cano, finally got back to Spain, 1,082 days after it left. It was the first ship to circumnavigate the world.

The arrangement of sails on a boat is called its rig. A square rig consists of sails hung on a boom across the boat (as in ancient Egyptian and Viking boats). This sort of rig cannot make the best use of wind blowing from side-on. The fore-and-aft rig, with a triangular sail hanging from a boom parallel with the boat's sides, is more effective. The Chinese had developed a similar rig on their early junks in about 500 B.C. It was developed in the Mediterranean in the third century A.D. In Europe in the fifteenth century, ships began to appear with a mixture of rigs—square-rigged sails on some masts and fore-and-aft rigs on others. Through the centuries, sailing ships grew larger, with more, taller masts and more sails on each one.

The fastest sailing ships were the "clippers," which had a huge sail area to take advantage of light winds, and streamlined hulls. They were used to carry important cargoes around the world, such as the new crop of tea from China to Europe.

Barques were high-capacity, multi-masted sailing ships that carried bulk cargoes such as grain between Europe, South America, and Australia. A small crew could operate the barque's simple rig. This particular barque, *France II*, built in 1911, was the biggest sailing ship ever built. Its steel hull was 416 feet (127 m) long.

STEAMSHIPS

DURING the nineteenth century, large sailing ships almost completely disappeared as steam power took over. The first successful steam-powered vessel was a river steamer built in the United States by Robert Fulton in 1808. On early steamships the steam engine turned paddle wheels that moved the ship along, but by the 1850s most ships were using propellers instead. Ocean-going steamships kept sails, too, because they could not carry enough coal or water for long-distance voyages, and their engines were not very reliable.

Fifteen hundred people lost their lives when the liner *Titanic* (*above*) sank after hitting an iceberg on its maiden voyage in 1912. Following the disaster, new safety regulations for ships were introduced.

One of the most important sea routes in the nineteenth century was across the Atlantic from Europe to the United States. Millions of people emigrated to the United States in ships. The first regular transatlantic service, starting in 1837, was the wooden paddle steamer *Great Western*, built by English engineer Isambard Kingdom Brunel. Larger and larger ships followed, including in 1858 Brunel's *Great Eastern*, easily the biggest ship in the world at the time, which could carry 4,000 passengers. Both passenger ships and merchant ships continued to increase in size, especially with the introduction of steel hulls in the late nineteenth century.

By the early twentieth century, huge luxury liners were crossing the Atlantic, and steam-powered merchant ships were carrying most of the world's cargo. The fastest liners used the new steam turbine engine, in which the steam turned a fan-like turbine, which turned the propellers at high speed.

The largest modern oil tankers (1), up to 1,476 feet (450 m) long, and known as ultra-large crude carriers (ULCCs), dwarf a 16th-century Spanish galleon (2).

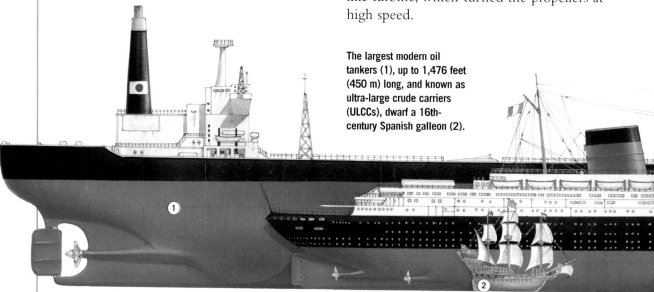

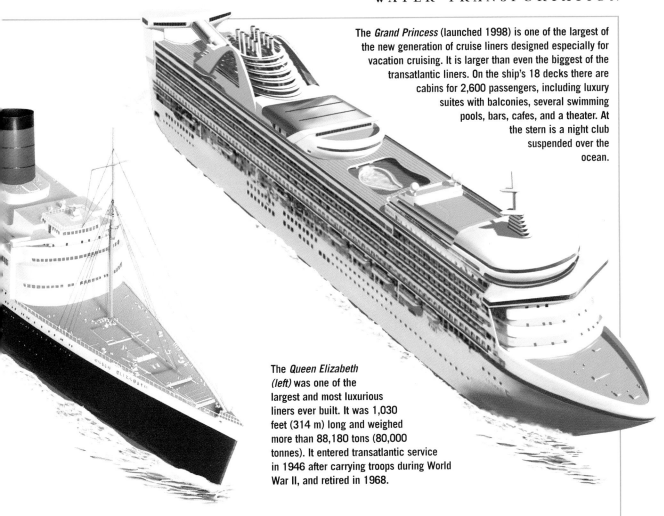

The *Grand Princess* (launched 1998) is one of the largest of the new generation of cruise liners designed especially for vacation cruising. It is larger than even the biggest of the transatlantic liners. On the ship's 18 decks there are cabins for 2,600 passengers, including luxury suites with balconies, several swimming pools, bars, cafes, and a theater. At the stern is a night club suspended over the ocean.

The *Queen Elizabeth* (left) was one of the largest and most luxurious liners ever built. It was 1,030 feet (314 m) long and weighed more than 88,180 tons (80,000 tonnes). It entered transatlantic service in 1946 after carrying troops during World War II, and retired in 1968.

In the middle of the twentieth century, steam power began to give way to diesel power. Diesel engines are smaller, cleaner, far more efficient, and need fewer crew to operate them. Steam had almost completely disappeared by the 1980s.

As air travel became convenient and cheap in the 1960s, passengers stopped traveling by sea and the age of the liner came to an end. But as cruise vacations became popular in the 1980s, construction of new, giant cruise liners began.

The French liner *Normandie* (3), launched in 1935, was nearly 1,000 feet (300 m) long, accommodated 1,975 passengers and needed 1,345 crew. It was the first of what were called the "1,000-foot" liners.

HMS *Dreadnought* (4), launched in 1906, was the first battleship driven by steam turbines.

GLOBTIK TOKYO

MODERN SHIPS

MODERN SHIPS and boats can be categorized by the the jobs they do. Merchant ships include cruise liners, ferries, cargo ships, and utility ships, such as dredgers and tugboats. Military ships include warships and support ships, called auxiliaries. There are also numerous different types of fishing boat and leisure craft, from luxury yachts to sailing dinghies.

Small cargoes are carried in standard-sized metal boxes called containers on container ships, which are loaded and unloaded at dedicated container terminals. Cargoes such as ores, coal, and grain are carried by bulk carriers. Oil and other liquids are carried by tankers.

The main part of a ship is its hull, the part that sits in the water. It keeps the ship watertight and forms a strong structure that supports the other parts of the ship and its cargo. Inside the hull are horizontal decks and vertical walls called bulkheads.

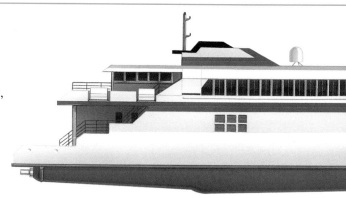

The SeaCat is a high-speed vehicle ferry. It is a catamaran, which means it has two hulls. Fast ferries like this are powered by gas turbine (jet) engines, giving them top speeds in excess of 40 knots (46 mph).

Different types of ship have their own specialized parts. For example, vehicle ferries called roll-on roll-off (ro-ro) ferries, designed for a quick turnaround in port, have huge bow or stern doors, and uncluttered decks where the vehicles park. Container ships have their own on-deck cranes for moving containers about. Aircraft carriers have a flat main deck that forms a runway where aircraft take off and land, with hangars underneath.

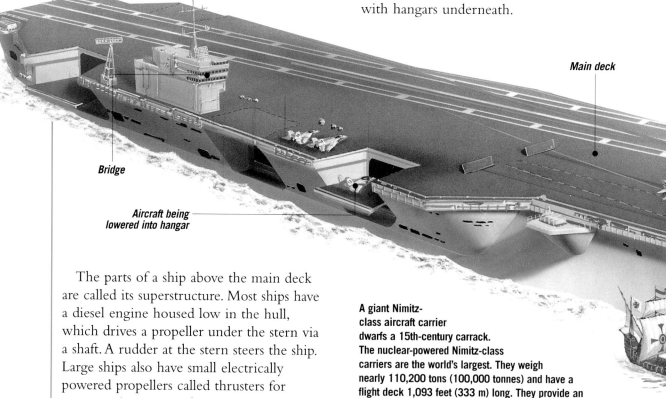

Main deck

Bridge

Aircraft being lowered into hangar

The parts of a ship above the main deck are called its superstructure. Most ships have a diesel engine housed low in the hull, which drives a propeller under the stern via a shaft. A rudder at the stern steers the ship. Large ships also have small electrically powered propellers called thrusters for maneuvering accurately in port.

A giant Nimitz-class aircraft carrier dwarfs a 15th-century carrack. The nuclear-powered Nimitz-class carriers are the world's largest. They weigh nearly 110,200 tons (100,000 tonnes) and have a flight deck 1,093 feet (333 m) long. They provide an operations base for nearly 100 attack aircraft.

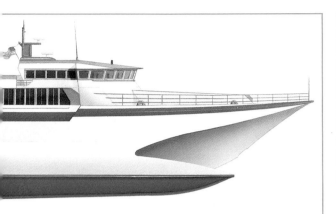

Ships are controlled from a room high up near the bow, called a bridge. From here, the crew navigate from place to place, using engine and steering controls, and keeping track of their position using charts, satellite navigation systems, lighthouses, and buoys. Radar helps to avoid collisions at night or in fog, and sonar warns of shallow water under the ship.

SUBMARINES

A SUBMARINE IS a vessel that can travel submerged under the water as well as on the surface. A submarine needs an extremely strong hull to resist the pressure deep underwater. Ballast tanks in the hull are filled with water to make the submarine heavier so that it dives. The tanks are "blown" with air to empty them and make the submarine surface again.

While submerged, submarines are propelled by battery-powered electric motors that do not produce dangerous exhaust fumes. On the surface, diesel engines take over. They recharge the batteries at the same time.

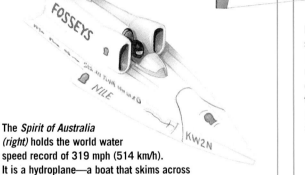

The *Spirit of Australia* (right) holds the world water speed record of 319 mph (514 km/h). It is a hydroplane—a boat that skims across the top of the water.

Huge military submarines such as USS *George Washington (above)* lurk under the water and attack enemy ships with torpedoes. Nuclear-powered submarines can stay submerged for months.

A submersible such as *Alvin (below)* is a miniature submarine. Submersibles are mostly used for research in the ocean depths. Robot submersibles also carry out underwater repairs on oil rigs.

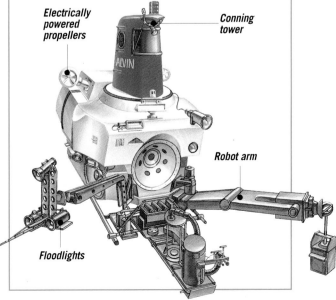

Electrically powered propellers

Conning tower

Robot arm

Floodlights

Santa Maria *(Columbus's ship) for scale comparison*

HISTORY OF CARS

PEOPLE had used carts pulled by horses, oxen, or other large animals for more than 5,000 years before the first self-propelled vehicle was built. This was a clumsy steam-powered carriage designed to pull artillery guns, built by Frenchman Nicolas Cugnot in 1769. Steam-powered vehicles called traction engines took the place of horses on farms from the 1850s. Cars driven by small steam engines were popular in the United States in the 1890s.

Nicolas Cugnot's steam carriage *(above)* could manage just 3.1 mph (5 km/h). Karl Benz's three-wheeled car *(right)*, which had a single-cylinder gasoline engine, reached speeds of 9.3 mph (15 km/h).

The age of the car really started with the development of the internal combustion engine. This development began in the 1850s, but it was not until the 1880s that small, lightweight, gasoline-driven engines were perfected, first by Gottlieb Daimler in Germany. The first gasoline-driven car was built by German engineer Karl Benz in 1885.

The first two strokes of the four-stroke cycle are the inlet stroke *(left)* and the compression stroke *(right)*.

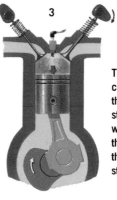

The cycle is completed by the ignition stroke *(left)*, which creates the power, and the exhaust stroke *(right)*.

INTERNAL COMBUSTION ENGINE

The job of the internal combustion engine is to convert the energy stored in its fuel into movement. Inside the heavy engine block are cylinders (normally four in a car engine). Pistons fit snugly inside the cylinders. When the engine is running, the pistons move up and down, turning a crankshaft (which turns the wheels) via connecting rods.

Most internal combustion engines work on a four-stroke cycle which is repeated again and again as the pistons move up and down. On the first stroke, as the piston moves down, the inlet valve opens to allow a mixture of fuel and air to be sucked into the cylinder (1). On the second stroke, as the piston moves up, the air and fuel is squeezed into the top of the cylinder (2). Now a spark is created electrically by the spark plug, igniting the fuel, which forces the cylinder down (3). This is the third stroke. On the fourth stroke, the exhaust valve opens to let waste gases be forced out as the piston moves up again (4).

Model-T Ford

Meanwhile, motor sports were becoming popular, with cars taking part in races and rallies, and car builders competing to build the world's fastest car. The land-speed record was first set in 1898, at 39 miles (63 km) per hour.

Early land-speed record-holders:
(1) *Jeantaud* (1899, 58.2 mph),
(2) *La Jamais Contente* (1899, 65.8 mph), (3) *Serpollet* (1902, 75 mph) and (4) *Mors* (1902, 77.1 mph).

THE MOTOR AGE BEGINS

Benz and Daimler started selling cars in the late 1890s. In 1891 the first car with a front engine and rear-wheel drive appeared. Early cars were tricky to operate, slow, and hand-built, which made them expensive. In 1908 motoring was opened up to ordinary people with the introduction in the United States of the Model-T Ford *(above)*. This small car was built on a production line, making it cheap to make and cheap to buy.

A street scene in Paris in 1910. As the number of cars on the streets grew, rules of the road had to be introduced to prevent the cars crashing into horses, pedestrians, or each other.

MODERN CARS

ALL MODERN CARS, from the smallest urban car to the fastest racing cars, have similar basic features. Wheels and suspension allow the car to roll smoothly along the road. Tires on the wheels grip the road surface, allowing the car to accelerate, brake, and corner without sliding.

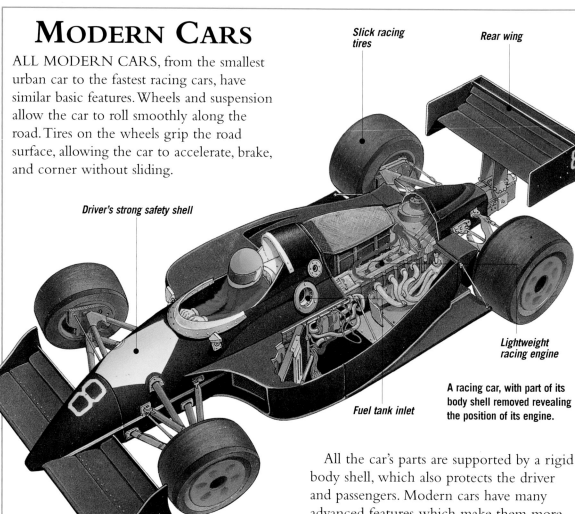

Slick racing tires

Rear wing

Driver's strong safety shell

Lightweight racing engine

Fuel tank inlet

A racing car, with part of its body shell removed revealing the position of its engine.

Front wing

Power from the engine is transferred to the wheels by the transmission, including the gears. The fuel and exhaust systems supply fuel to the engine and carry away waste gases. The electrical system supplies electricity to the engine's spark plugs, the car's lights, and other electrical gadgets.

All the car's parts are supported by a rigid body shell, which also protects the driver and passengers. Modern cars have many advanced features which make them more efficient, and easier and safer to drive. These include computerized engine-management systems which control the flow of fuel to the engine, navigation computers which give the driver directions, antilock brakes which prevent skidding, and air bags which protect the driver in an accident. Many of these features were originally developed to improve the performance of racing cars, but have become standard on road cars.

A stretch limousine *(below)* is a chauffeur-driven luxury car used for special occasions such as weddings. Inside are large, comfortable seats, where passengers can enjoy drinks from a bar and even watch television.

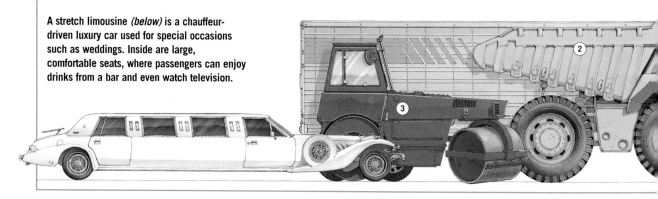

AERODYNAMICS

The way air flows around a moving body is called aerodynamics. As cars move along, the air flowing around them tries to slow them down. The effect is called drag, and it prevents cars from continuing to speed up. The more streamlined the shape of a car, the lower the drag on it, and so the faster its top speed. Racing cars *(left)* have special aerodynamic features, such as wings that create downforce. These force a car's tires onto the road, increasing grip and allowing the car to corner more quickly without skidding sideways.

Aerodynamics are especially important in very high-speed cars, such as *Thrust SSC*, which holds the land-speed record of 762.9 mph (1227.723 km/h). It is the only car to have gone faster than sound.

All road vehicles have similar features to cars, but the features are often specialized. For example, large haulage trucks (1) have many wheels to spread their heavy load. Off-road vehicles, such as dumper trucks (2), have large wheels with chunky tires for good grip in the mud. Road-rollers (3) have solid steel wheels.

BICYCLES

Macmillan's pedal bicycle   Michaux's "boneshaker"   Starley's modern bicycle

A BICYCLE is a human-powered vehicle with two wheels. The first bicycles, called "hobby horses," were built about 200 years ago. The rider moved along by pushing his or her feet against the ground. The first pedal-powered bicycle was made by Scottish blacksmith Kirkpatrick Macmillan in 1839. In 1861 in Paris, Pierre Michaux built a bicycle on which the pedals turned the front wheels. It was known as the "boneshaker" and was the first popular bicycle. The modern bicycle, with a diamond-shaped frame and chain-driven back wheel, was designed in 1885 by Englishman John Starley.

MOTORCYCLES

Early motorcycles were simply bicycles with a small steam engine attached, but they were not practical machines. The first modern-style motorcycles, with a metal frame, two air-filled tires and a lightweight gasoline engine, appeared around 1900. Modern motorcycles have similar features to cars, but have much greater acceleration.

STORY OF FLIGHT 1

FOR THOUSANDS of years, people must have watched birds flying around them and dreamed of copying them. Many actually tried it. These "birdmen" strapped on wings and leaped from towers, trying to flap their arms. Most were killed.

The first manned flight took place in Paris in 1783, in a hot-air balloon built by the French brothers Joseph and Etienne Montgolfier. Aviators also began to develop airships—balloons with a streamlined shape, pushed through the air by an engine. Balloons and airships are described as lighter-than-air aircraft because they float upward in the heavier air around them.

The first heavier-than-air aircraft were gliders, built and flown in the nineteenth century by pioneers such as the German Otto Lilienthal. In the United States, two brothers, Orville and Wilbur Wright, were experimenting with kites and gliders. They made thousands of test flights in their gliders, gradually perfecting their controls. In 1903 they finally built an airplane, called *Flyer 1*, with a gasoline engine. It made the first-ever powered, controlled airplane flight, which lasted just 12 seconds *(below)*.

The Montgolfiers' balloon *(above)* carried the first pilot and passenger on a 25-minute flight. The air in the balloon was heated by straw burning on the ground. In 1852 Frenchman Henry Giffard took off in his steam-powered airship *(above right)*. The envelope was filled with lighter-than-air hydrogen gas rather than hot air. Airships such as the 803-foot (245-m)-long *Graf Zeppelin II (right)* had a steel skeleton covered in fabric. The gas was contained in huge bags inside.

The Blériot XI, in which Louis Blériot crossed the English Channel in 1909.

In the decade after the Wright brothers' historic flight, aviation became a popular sport. Race meetings and airshows were held, and pilots made historic long-distance flights. Aircraft technology steadily improved. Aviators began to understand how to build stronger aircraft structures without increasing weight, wings which gave better lift and created less drag, and controls that made life easier for the pilot. The standard aircraft shape, with a tail section supporting a fin and tailplane, began to become popular. More efficient and powerful engines and propellers gave aircraft greater speed, endurance, and reliability. By 1913 the speed record was 126 miles (203 km) per hour, and the distance record 634 miles (1,021 km).

The Sikorsky *Le Grand* (above), the first four-engined airplane, and the Spad S.XIII World War I fighter (right).

Armies began ordering aircraft from manufacturers such as Glenn Curtiss in the United States and Louis Blériot in France. During World War I, aircraft became specialized for certain jobs, such as fast, maneuverable fighters and large, long-distance bombers. Large, flat decks were added to some battleships where aircraft could take off to attack enemy ships with torpedoes.

HELICOPTERS

THE IDEA of a flying machine lifted by a spinning rotor is centuries' old. The Italian painter and scientist Leonardo da Vinci designed a simple helicopter in about 1500, but he did not have an engine to power it. In 1907 Frenchman Paul Cornu rose 12 inches (30 cm) into the air in a twin-rotor helicopter, but he had no controls.

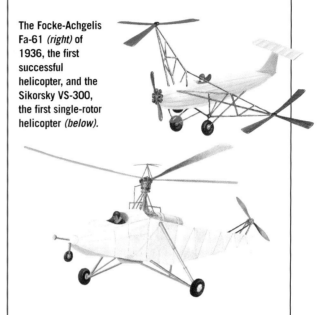

The Focke-Achgelis Fa-61 (right) of 1936, the first successful helicopter, and the Sikorsky VS-300, the first single-rotor helicopter (below).

The first successful helicopters, built in the 1930s, had two rotors for lift and a propeller for propulsion. The single-rotor helicopter was developed by Russian-born American engineer Igor Sikorsky. The main rotor provided lift and propulsion, and the tail rotor prevented the fuselage (body of the aircraft) spinning in the opposite direction to the main rotor. Helicopters were soon being used by navies and for passenger services. The development of the jet engine in the 1950s made larger, faster helicopters possible.

Westland Sea King

STORY OF FLIGHT II

THE FIRST PASSENGER airlines were formed in 1919, just after the end of World War I. Their airliners were converted wartime bombers, such as the Farman Goliath, which had seats for 11 passengers. Flying in them was cold and bumpy, and there was noise and vibration from the piston engines. In the 1920s and 1930s aviation engineers began building in metal instead of wood, creating aircraft with strong tubular fuselages and monoplane wings, such as the Martin B-10 bomber.

The first modern-style airliners, such as the Douglas DC-3, appeared in the mid-1930s. During World War II pilots needed heavy bombers, such as the B-24 Liberator, and fast fighters, such as the Ilyushin Il-2.

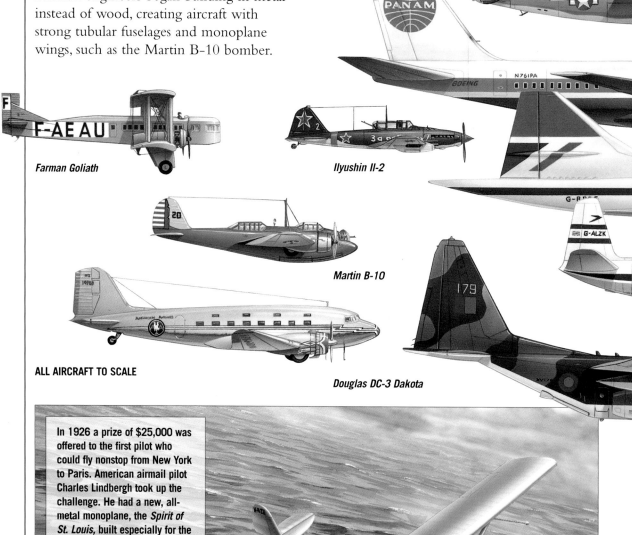

Farman Goliath

Ilyushin Il-2

Martin B-10

ALL AIRCRAFT TO SCALE

Douglas DC-3 Dakota

In 1926 a prize of $25,000 was offered to the first pilot who could fly nonstop from New York to Paris. American airmail pilot Charles Lindbergh took up the challenge. He had a new, all-metal monoplane, the *Spirit of St. Louis,* built especially for the journey, and decided to fly on his own. Lindbergh took off from New York on May 19, 1927. Navigating virtually by guesswork, flying low to avoid fog, and fighting sleep, Lindbergh reached Paris 33 hours and 30 minutes later, to achieve the first solo Atlantic

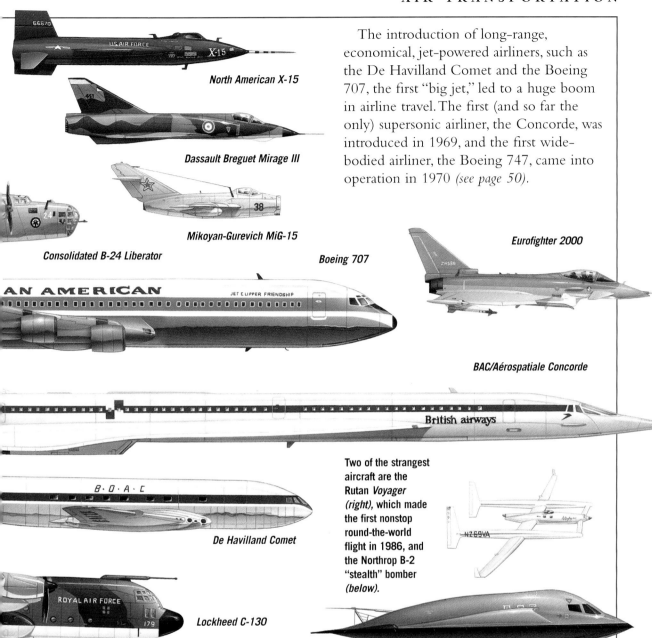

North American X-15

Dassault Breguet Mirage III

Mikoyan-Gurevich MiG-15

Consolidated B-24 Liberator

Boeing 707

Eurofighter 2000

BAC/Aérospatiale Concorde

British airways

De Havilland Comet

Lockheed C-130

Two of the strangest aircraft are the Rutan *Voyager (right)*, which made the first nonstop round-the-world flight in 1986, and the Northrop B-2 "stealth" bomber *(below)*.

The introduction of long-range, economical, jet-powered airliners, such as the De Havilland Comet and the Boeing 707, the first "big jet," led to a huge boom in airline travel. The first (and so far the only) supersonic airliner, the Concorde, was introduced in 1969, and the first wide-bodied airliner, the Boeing 747, came into operation in 1970 *(see page 50)*.

JET AIRCRAFT

The jet engine was developed in the late 1930s, both by Hans von Ohain in Germany and Frank Whittle in Britain. The first jet aircraft flew in 1939. Jet engines powered new jet fighters with swept-back wings, such as the MiG-15 and later the Mirage, and a new generation of airliners. Rocket-powered aircraft such as the X-15 were built for research into high-speed flight. The X-15 still holds the world speed record of 4,520 miles (7,274 km) per hour.

The latest airliners, fighters such as the Eurofighter, and bombers such as the Northrop B-2, have sophisticated control systems, such as "fly-by-wire." In an aircraft with a fly-by-wire system, the pilot controls where the aircraft goes, but a computer actually does the flying. In an airliner, fly-by-wire can prevent the pilot making mistakes such as stalling. In a fighter, it allows the pilot to make maneuvers that would be impossible if he or she were using a standard mechanical control system.

BOEING 747

ALL MODERN airplanes have similar features, although those of airliners such as the Boeing 747 are larger and more complex than those of smaller airplanes. The fuselage is a strong tube inside which the passengers, crew, and their baggage travel. Wings support the airplane in the air by creating a force called lift. Engines *(see page 53)* provide a forward force called thrust, which pushes the airplane forward against the resistance of the air (which is called drag). The fin and tailplane keep the plane flying straight and level. Hinged sections called control surfaces (the rudder, elevators, and ailerons) steer the aircraft through the air.

The Boeing 747-400, shown here, is the latest model of the world's largest airliner, known as the "jumbo jet." It can carry up to 569 passengers (but normally carries 420 in first, business, and economy cabins), and cruises at up to 612 miles (985 km) per hour, at an altitude of 6.2 miles (10 km). Its maximum range is 87,610 miles (14,100 km)—more than a third of the way round the world.

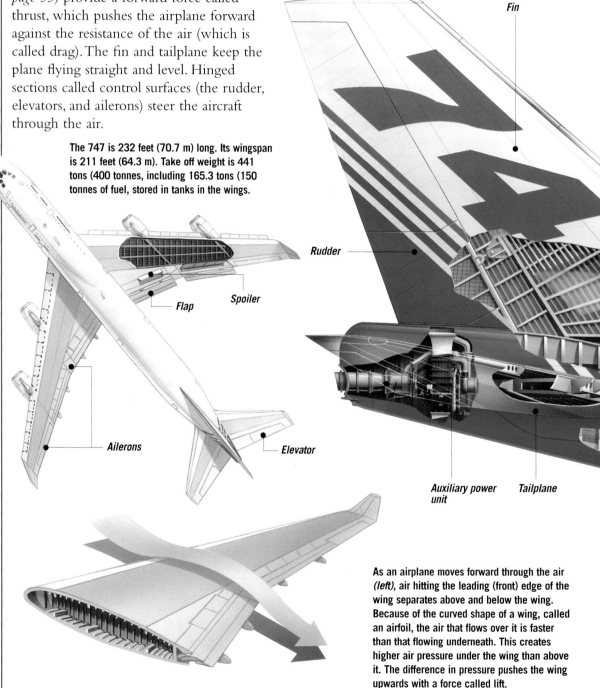

The 747 is 232 feet (70.7 m) long. Its wingspan is 211 feet (64.3 m). Take off weight is 441 tons (400 tonnes, including 165.3 tons (150 tonnes of fuel, stored in tanks in the wings.

Flap

Spoiler

Ailerons

Elevator

Fin

Rudder

Auxiliary power unit

Tailplane

As an airplane moves forward through the air *(left)*, air hitting the leading (front) edge of the wing separates above and below the wing. Because of the curved shape of a wing, called an airfoil, the air that flows over it is faster than that flowing underneath. This creates higher air pressure under the wing than above it. The difference in pressure pushes the wing upwards with a force called lift.

At low speed during take-off and landing, flaps (1) extend from the trailing (rear) edge of the wing. On the 747, each set of flaps has three sections. There are also small flaps on the leading edge of the wing (2). Flaps increase the size of the wing, and so create extra lift. For take-off *(left)*, flaps are partly extended. For landing *(below)* they are fully extended. Spoilers (3) flip up from the upper surface of the wing. They break the flow of air over the wing, reducing lift.

CONTROLLING LIFT

The amount of lift from a wing increases with the airplane's speed and also with the angle of attack, the angle at which the wing hits the air. At lower speeds, the pilot maintains lift by raising the nose of the plane to increase the angle of attack. But if the angle becomes too great, air cannot flow smoothly over the top of the wing and lift is lost. This is called a stall.

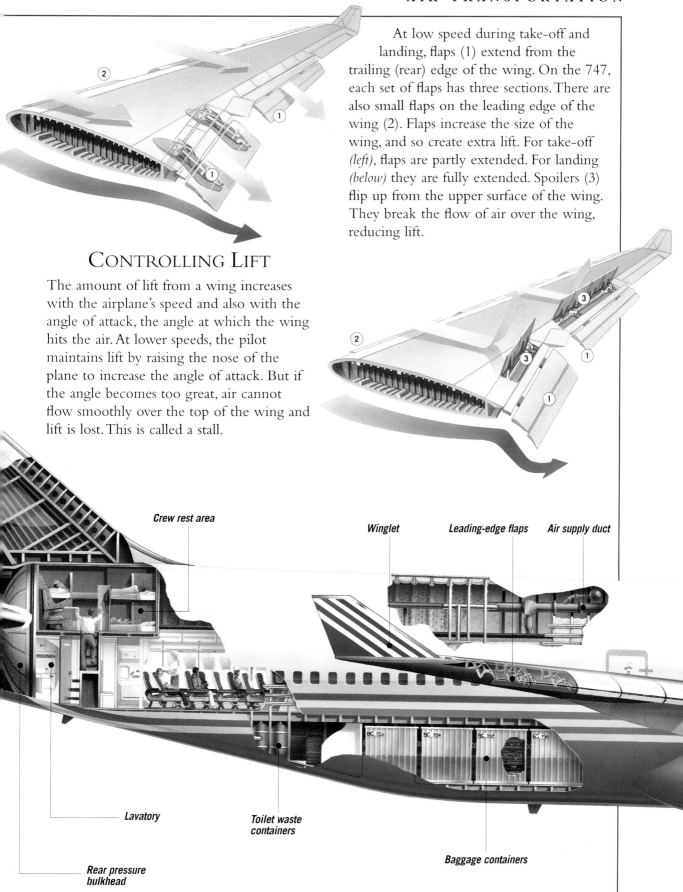

Crew rest area

Winglet

Leading-edge flaps

Air supply duct

Lavatory

Toilet waste containers

Baggage containers

Rear pressure bulkhead

INSIDE AN AIRLINER

SEATED AT THE controls on the flight deck are the pilot and copilot. For much of the journey, the controls are switched to an automatic control system, or autopilot. This uses computers to sense outside conditions, such as wind speed, and to manipulate the controls accordingly to travel along a preset route. All the crew have to do is to keep an eye on the monitors to check that all systems are functioning correctly.

For safety reasons, a Boeing 747 is equipped with a voice recorder and a flight recorder, sometimes known as the "black box" (although it is actually a bright orange color). These instruments record every maneuver the aircraft makes. In the event of an accident or a crash, the recordings can be played back and provide evidence for what went wrong.

Six display screens—three for each pilot—give all the information needed to fly the plane. The Primary Flight Display (1) shows the airplane's attitude—the angle at

A Boeing 747's flight deck controls

which it is flying in relation to the earth. It also indicates the plane's course, its speed and the height of the plane above the land or sea. The Navigation Display (2) plots the plane's position on a map of the route. The Engine Indication and Crew Alerting System (EICAS) (3) gives information about the operation of the airplane's systems and engines.

Air pressure, which keeps oxygen supplied to our lungs, is much lower at cruising altitudes (about 32,000 feet [10,000 m]). Air is pumped into the pressurized passenger cabin to keep it at comfortable levels.

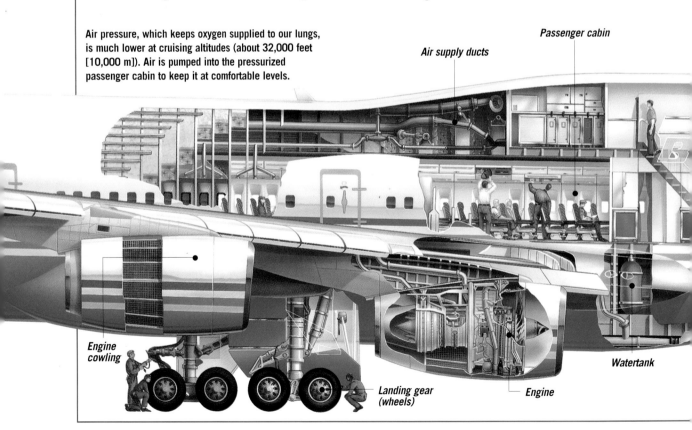

Passenger cabin

Air supply ducts

Engine cowling

Landing gear (wheels)

Engine

Watertank

In a jet engine *(right),* air is drawn in (1), compressed by spinning blades (2), mixed with kerosene fuel, and burned in a combustion chamber (3). The hot exhaust gas escapes through the rear of the engine, turning a turbine (4) (which drives the compressor) as it spurts past. The backward-flowing air (5) provides a forward thrust, like the kick of a rifle after a bullet is fired.

JET ENGINES

There are four engines on a Boeing 747, two on each wing, contained within engine cowlings (casings) attached to the wing undersides. The front entrance to the engine, known as the intake, is so large a person could stand in it.

The 747 engine is a type of jet engine called a turbofan. All jets work in the same way: Hot, compressed air is expelled from the back of the engine, driving it forward (see illustration above). In a turbofan, air is sucked into the engine by a whirling fan (6) in front of the compressor. It is driven by another turbine at the rear of the engine.

Some of the inflowing air is ducted around the combustion chamber to join the exhaust gas. Besides being much more powerful than other types, the engine is cooler and quieter, and more economical in its use of fuel.

Turbofan engines are equipped with thrust reversers. When in use, the jet of hot exhaust gases is deflected forward instead of backward, producing a force which rapidly slows down the plane landing on the runway.

Besides driving the plane through the air, the engines supply the power needed for the electricity used on board. Air is also diverted from the engine compressor to pressurize the cabin.

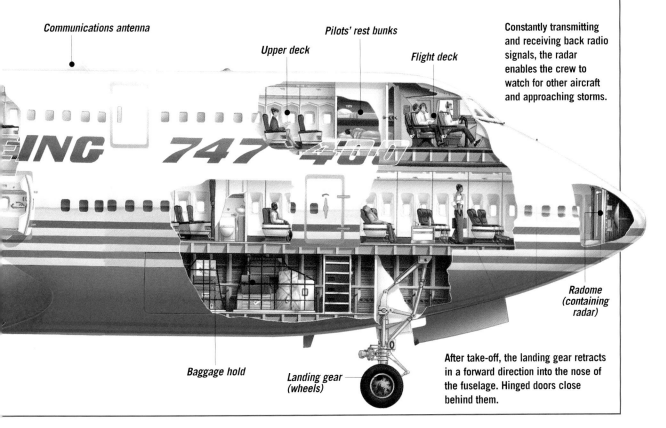

Communications antenna

Upper deck

Pilots' rest bunks

Flight deck

Constantly transmitting and receiving back radio signals, the radar enables the crew to watch for other aircraft and approaching storms.

Baggage hold

Landing gear (wheels)

Radome (containing radar)

After take-off, the landing gear retracts in a forward direction into the nose of the fuselage. Hinged doors close behind them.

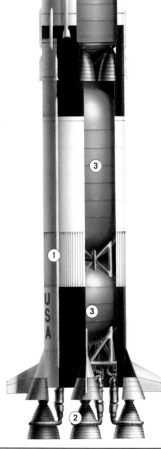

SPACE TRAVEL I

ALTHOUGH SPACE starts just 62 miles (100 km) above the earth's surface, it is very difficult to get there. Airplanes cannot reach space because the air gets thinner and thinner with altitude. Their wings begin to lose lift and their jet engines stop working through lack of oxygen. So spacecraft need rocket engines that work in the vacuum of space. To travel in space, a spacecraft must reach a speed of 17,710 miles (28,500 km) per hour, the minimum speed required to escape the pull of the earth's gravity. Once in space, the craft's engines can be turned off. It maintains its speed because there is no air to slow it down.

In a rocket engine, two different fuels mix and react together inside a combustion chamber, creating hot gases that rush out of a nozzle at great speed. The gases rushing in one direction push the engine and the spacecraft in the opposite direction. The first experimental rocket was launched in 1926 by the American inventor Robert Goddard, but it was not until the 1950s that a rocket powerful enough to reach space was developed. Spacecraft are normally carried into space by rocket-powered launch vehicles, which are huge compared to the spacecraft. For example, the 154-ton (140-tonne) *Apollo* spacecraft needed a 3,300 ton(3000-tonne) Saturn V rocket to launch it. Most of the weight was fuel.

The enormous Saturn V, built to launch the *Apollo* series of spacecraft *(see opposite)*, consisted of three rocket stages. In a multistage rocket, the engines of each stage fire until their fuel runs out. Then the stage is jettisoned (cast off) and the engines of the next stage fire. The rocket gets lighter each time a stage is lost, allowing it to accelerate more easily. This is more efficient than one rocket.

The first stage (1) of a Saturn V had five engines (2) fueled by kerosene and liquid oxygen stored in huge tanks (3). It created as much thrust as 50 jumbo jets. The second stage (4) also had five engines, fueled by liquid hydrogen and oxygen. The third stage (5) had one engine, also fueled by liquid hydrogen and oxygen.

On top of the 364-foot (111-m) rocket were the lunar module (6), service module (7) and command module (8) of the *Apollo* spacecraft, and an escape rocket (9), that pulled the command module clear of the rocket in case of an emergency during launch.

Robert Goddard's first rocket *(below, left)* reached an altitude of just 41 feet (12.5 m). The German V2 long-range rocket *(center)* was built as a weapon from 1942. The Soviet Vostok launcher *(right)* launched the first-ever satellite, *Sputnik 1 (left)*.

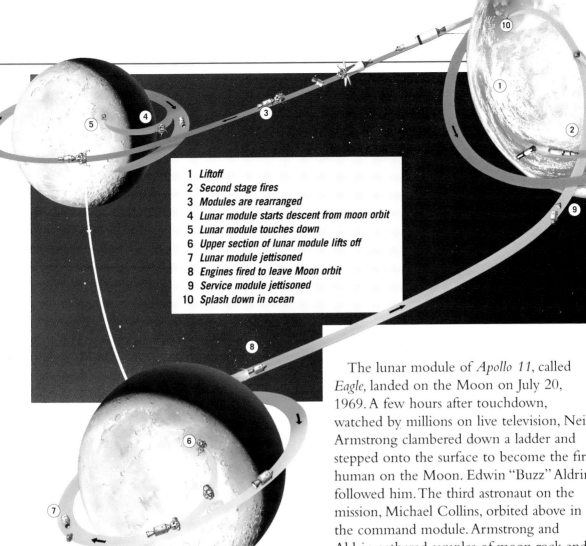

1. Liftoff
2. Second stage fires
3. Modules are rearranged
4. Lunar module starts descent from moon orbit
5. Lunar module touches down
6. Upper section of lunar module lifts off
7. Lunar module jettisoned
8. Engines fired to leave Moon orbit
9. Service module jettisoned
10. Splash down in ocean

THE MOON MISSIONS

After the former Soviet Union launched the first man into orbit in 1961, President John F. Kennedy announced that the United States would land a man on the moon before the end of the 1960s. A new spacecraft specially designed for the mission, called Apollo, was built. It consisted of a command module, from where the astronauts controlled the craft, a service module, which contained a rocket engine and life-support systems, and a lunar module, the only section that was to descend to the Moon's surface. A new launch vehicle, the giant Saturn V, was also built. During a series of missions in Earth and Moon orbit throughout the 1960s, Apollo was thoroughly tested and astronauts trained for the Moon landing.

The lunar module of *Apollo 11*, called *Eagle,* landed on the Moon on July 20, 1969. A few hours after touchdown, watched by millions on live television, Neil Armstrong clambered down a ladder and stepped onto the surface to become the first human on the Moon. Edwin "Buzz" Aldrin followed him. The third astronaut on the mission, Michael Collins, orbited above in the command module. Armstrong and Aldrin gathered samples of moon rock and soil *(below)* and planted a flag before lifting off in the upper section of the lunar module to dock with the command module. There they rejoined Collins, jettisoned the lunar module and began the return trip to Earth. Five more Apollo moon missions followed, the last in 1972.

SPACE TRAVEL II

SINCE the Apollo moon missions were completed in 1972, no astronauts have been further than Earth orbit, but many unmanned spacecraft, called space probes, have visited the other planets in our solar system. Probes carry cameras and sensing equipment that send back photographs and other data. Some probes actually land on the planets' surfaces. Hundreds of satellites for communications *(see pages 14, 16 and 19),* weather forecasting, scientific research, and astronomy *(see page 27),* have also been launched into Earth orbit.

The first permanent space station, *Salyut 1,* was launched in 1971. Inside space stations, astronauts carry out experiments to see how people react to staying in space for long periods, and how plants and animals cope with very low gravity. Probes, satellites, space stations, and their crews are lifted into space by launch vehicles such as the European Ariane space rocket, or by the American space shuttle.

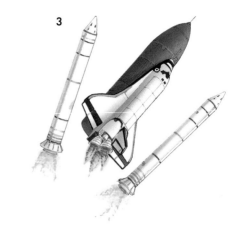

Soon after lift-off (2), the shuttle turns onto its back. The booster rockets last for two minutes, then separate from the fuel tank (3) and parachute back to Earth for reuse. The fuel in the external tank runs out after nine minutes, after which the orbiter jettisons it (4) and it falls back into the atmosphere, where it burns up because of the intense heat created. The orbiter is now on its own. The OMS engines are fired for a short time to accelerate the orbiter into its correct orbit.

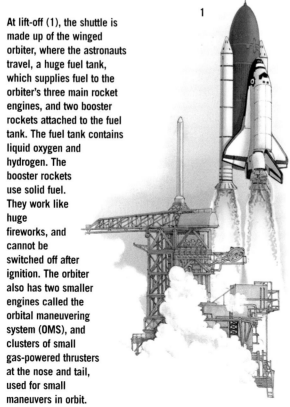

At lift-off (1), the shuttle is made up of the winged orbiter, where the astronauts travel, a huge fuel tank, which supplies fuel to the orbiter's three main rocket engines, and two booster rockets attached to the fuel tank. The fuel tank contains liquid oxygen and hydrogen. The booster rockets use solid fuel. They work like huge fireworks, and cannot be switched off after ignition. The orbiter also has two smaller engines called the orbital maneuvering system (OMS), and clusters of small gas-powered thrusters at the nose and tail, used for small maneuvers in orbit.

The space shuttle was designed as a re-usable spacecraft because of the huge cost of rockets and craft such as the Saturn V and Apollo, all the parts of which were completely destroyed during a mission. The shuttle flies into space like a rocket and glides back to Earth like an airplane.

During "extra-vehicular activity" outside their spacecraft *(right),* astronauts are protected from the cold, high-speed meteorites, and radiation from the Sun by a complex spacesuit. Astronauts sometimes use a manned-maneuvering unit (MMU), powered by tiny gas jets, which allows them to maneuver freely in space.

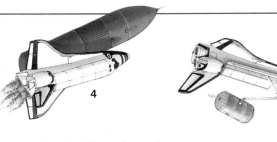

FUTURE SPACE TRAVEL

At the beginning of the twenty-first century, traveling even to Earth's closest neighbor planet Mars, let alone planets in other solar systems, is still impractical. A trip to Mars and back would take more than a year. The equipment, supplies, and fuel for such a trip would require a vast rocket to launch a spacecraft from Earth. A return trip to the outer planets would take a lifetime without some new form of propulsion with much greater power than a rocket engine. For the time being, space probes remain the best way of exploring distant worlds.

Less than fifteen minutes after launch, the shuttle is in orbit at an altitude of about 124 miles (200 km). Now the astronauts can carry out their mission—in this case, launching a satellite from the payload bay (in the upper part of the orbiter's fuselage) using the orbiter's remotely controlled robot arm (5). With the mission complete, the OMS engines slow down the orbiter so that it begins to fall back to Earth (6).

Work is under way on a new international space station, which will be a base for scientific research. It is a modular structure, being built in space module-by-module, with sections being delivered into orbit by the shuttle and unmanned launch vehicles. In the future, space stations such as this, or permanent bases on the Moon, could be a starting point for space journeys. Spacecraft would be built and launched from there rather than from Earth.

During reentry into the atmosphere, heat-resistant ceramic tiles protect the orbiter from the intense heat. It gradually slows as it descends, and finally glides back onto a runway like an airplane (7).

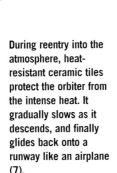

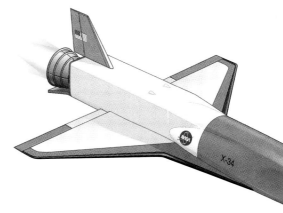

The whole shuttle, except for the large fuel tank, which is destroyed during launch, can be reused. The first shuttle mission was flown by the shuttle *Columbia* in 1981. Since then, there have been dozens of missions to launch or repair satellites, service space stations, and carry out scientific and military research.

New types of reusable vehicles, called spaceplanes, which will carry supplies to space stations, are under development. They will take off and gain altitude like airplanes, with their engines working like jet engines, and then make the jump to orbit with their engines working like rocket engines. Spaceplanes could also make passenger flights, cutting the journey time between Europe and Australia to under two hours. The international space station will have a spaceplane "lifeboat" for the crew.

TIMELINE

c.3500 B.C. The first known sailing boats are built by the ancient Egyptians.

c.3500 The solid wheel is developed in Asia and is used on wheeled carts.

c. 3000 The abacus is invented in Asia.

c. 500 Chinese shipbuilders invent the fore-and-aft sailing rig.

A.D. 50 Hero of Alexandria invents a simple steam-powered machine.

c.650 Printing with ink-covered carved wooden blocks is developed in China.

c.1000 The camera obscura is developed.

c.1100 The magnetic compass is being used for navigation in China.

1400s Three-masted ocean-going sailing ships are built in Europe.

1440 Johannes Gutenberg (Germany) invents the printing press.

1519–1522 One ship of an expedition led by Ferdinand Magellan (Portugal) is the first ship to sail around the world.

1590 Zacharias Janssen (Netherlands) builds the first compound microscope.

1609 Galileo Galilei (Italy) discovers four moons of Jupiter with a refracting telescope.

1642 Blaise Pascal (France) invents a mechanical calculating machine.

1688 The reflecting telescope is invented by Isaac Newton (England).

1698 Thomas Savery (England) builds a steam-powered pump designed to pump water from mines.

1712 Thomas Newcomen (England) completes a steam engine that is used to pump water from mines.

1765 James Watt (Scotland) builds a steam engine that becomes popular for powering industrial machinery.

1769 Nicolas Cugnot (France) builds a steam-powered gun carriage.

1783 The first manned flight takes place in a hot-air balloon built by the Montgolfier brothers (France).

1800 Alessandro Volta (Italy) invents the electric battery.

1801 Joseph Marie Jacquard (France) builds a loom controlled by punched cards.

1804 The first steam locomotive is built by Richard Trevithick (England).

1808 Robert Fulton (United States) builds the first successful steam-powered boat.

1827 Joseph Niépce takes the earliest-surviving photograph.

1828 The Stockton and Darlington passenger railway, England, opens.

1831 Michael Faraday invents the dynamo.

1832 Charles Babbage (England) patents a mechanical general-purpose computer.

1837 Samuel Morse (United States) develops an electric telegraph that uses Morse code.

1837 The steamship *Great Western* begins regular transatlantic passenger services.

1839 Kirkpatrick Macmillan (Scotland) builds the first pedal-powered bicycle.

1852 Henry Giffard (France) makes the first flight in a steam-powered airship.

1859 Jean-Joseph-Etienne Lenoir (France) invents the internal combustion engine.

1867 Christopher Scholes (United States) invents the typewriter with a QWERTY keyboard.

1868 The Michaux brothers (France) build a simple motorcycle.

1876 Alexander Graham Bell (United States) patents the telephone receiver.

1877 Thomas Edison demonstrates the phonograph, which records sound.

1878 The first telephone exchange opens.

1878 An electric railway is demonstrated in Germany.

1885 Karl Benz (Germany) builds the first car with a petrol engine.

1885 The modern bicycle shape is designed by John Starley (England).

1888 Heinrich Hertz (Germany) proves the existence of radio waves.

1888 John Boyd Dunlop (Scotland) invents the air-filled pneumatic tire.

1891 The first cars with a front engine and rear-wheel drive appear.

1892 Rudolf Diesel (Germany) invents the diesel engine.

1898 The first practical submarine is built by John Holland (United States).

1901 Guglielmo Marconi (Italy) sends a message across the Atlantic by radio.

1903 *Flyer 1*, built by the Wright brothers (United States), makes the first controlled, powered flight by a heavier-than-air craft.

1904 John Fleming (England) invents the diode valve.

1907 Paul Cornu (France) makes a small hop in a twin-rotor helicopter.

1926 Robert Goddard (United States) launches the first experimental liquid-fueled rocket.

1926 Television is demonstrated by John Logie Baird (Scotland).

1927 Charles Lindbergh (United States) makes the first nonstop transatlantic flight.

1932 The first electron microscope is built.

1936 Television broadcasting begins.

1936 The Focke-Achgelis Fa-61 is the first successful helicopter.

1939 The Heinkel He178 is the first jet-powered aircraft to fly.

1940s Electronic computers are developed. The first successful machine is the ENIAC.

1948 A transistor is developed in the United States.

1953 Color television broadcasting begins.

1955 The first hovercraft is built by Christopher Cockerell (England).

1957 *Sputnik 1*, the first artificial satellite, is put into orbit by the former USSR.

1959 The first integrated circuit is built in the United States by Texas Instruments.

1960 Theodore Maiman (United States) builds the first laser.

1962 The *Telstar* satellite transmits live television pictures across the Atlantic.

1965 In Japan, high-speed *shinkansen* "bullet" trains start operating on purpose-built tracks.

1969 The first astronauts land on the Moon in the *Apollo 11* mission.

1969 The first supersonic airliner Concorde makes its first flight.

1970 The Boeing 747 flies for the first time.

1971 The *Salyut 1* space station is launched.

1971 Intel builds the first microprocessor.

1979 Cell phones are introduced in Sweden.

1981 The space shuttle, the world's first reusable spaceship, enters service (United States).

1983 IBM launches its personal computer.

1985 CD-ROMs are introduced in Japan.

1988 The computerized "fly-by-wire" Airbus A320 airliner enters service.

1990 The Hubble Space Telescope is launched into orbit.

1990 The French TGV electric express train achieves a world-record speed of 320 mph.

1994 The Internet is opened to ordinary computer users.

1997 The *Pathfinder* probe lands on Mars.

GLOSSARY

Amplifier An electronic circuit that increases the strength of an electrical signal.

Amplify To make larger.

Amplitude The strength of a wave.

Analog Describes information that can have any value in a range, such as the height of a person.

Binary A number system that uses only the digits zero and one.

Carrier signal An electrical or radio wave that is shaped by modulation to create a signal for transmission.

Condense To turn from gas to liquid.

Diesel engine A type of internal combustion engine that ignites its fuel (diesel oil) by compressing it with air.

Digital Describes information made up of binary numbers only.

Digital electronics Electronic circuits in which information is represented in binary using currents that are either on or off.

Diode A semiconductor device that allows an electric current in one direction only.

Electrical or **electronic signal** An electric current that represents information, such as sound, by continuously changing in strength and direction.

Electrode A device on an electronic circuit, made of carbon or metal, that releases or accepts electrons.

Electron An extremely tiny particle that is part of an atom. An electric current is a stream of electrons.

Electronic circuit An electric circuit in which the flow of current is controlled by the circuit's components.

Electronics The study of how electrons (which make up electric currents) behave and their application in electronic circuits.

Filter A colored, transparent piece of glass or plastic that allows light of its own color to pass through but stops other colors.

Frame An individual image or photograph in a series of images or photographs that makes up a moving picture, such as a television picture or movie film.

Frequency The number of wave crests that pass a point every second.

Friction A force that resists (acts against) the movement of one surface against another.

Gasoline engine A type of internal combustion engine that ignites its fuel (diesel oil) by compressing a mixture of fuel and air.

Generator A device similar to an electric motor, but which turns rotary movement into an electric current.

Hardware The physical parts of a computer, such as the electronic circuits, the disc drives, keyboard, and monitor.

Image A picture of an object or scene formed by focusing the rays of light coming from the object or scene.

Infrared radiation Invisible radiation similar to light which lies just to the left of visible light on the electromagnetic spectrum.

Insulator A material that reduces or stops the flow of heat or electricity.

Integrated circuit A complete electronic circuit consisting of microscopic electronic components built into a small piece of semiconducting material. Also known as a microchip or a silicon chip.

Internal combustion engine A type of engine in which the fuel such as gasoline or kerosene is burned inside the engine rather than outside.

Internet A huge computer network that links millions of computers around the world.

Jet engine An engine in which the burning fuel spins a fan (called a turbine) that creates a stream of hot gases from the rear of the engine.

Laser A device that creates an intense, parallel beam of light known as a laser beam.

Lens A shaped piece of glass or plastic that is used to focus light.

Lift The upward force created by an airplane's wings that counteracts gravity.

Microphone An electronic device that turns the pattern of a sound wave into an electric signal.

Microwaves High-frequency radio waves used in communications and for cooking.

Modulation The shaping of a wave, such as a changing electric current, radio wave or beam of light so that it represents information.

Monitor The screen of a computer, where text and graphics appear.

Pixel Short for picture element, which is one of the tiny colored dots that make up an image on a computer monitor.

Propeller A fan-like object that pushes against water (on a boat) or air (on an aircraft) as it spins at high speed.

Radar (RAdio **D**etection **A**nd **R**anging) A system that detects objects by transmitting radio waves and receiving the "echoes."

Radiation The emission and transfer through space of electromagnetic waves, including light, radio, X rays, etc.

Radio The use of radio waves for communication. Also the general broadcasting of sound and music.

Radio waves Invisible waves that are part of the electromagnetic spectrum and which travel at the speed of light.

Receiver A device that detects signals, such as radio waves.

Rocket engine An engine that creates a stream of hot gases by burning fuel in a chamber.

Satellite A spacecraft that orbits Earth. Communications satellites relay radio signals between ground stations on Earth's surface.

Semiconductor A substance that can act both as a conductor of electricity and as an insulator.

Software The programs and data that a computer uses and stores.

Steam engine An engine that uses pressurized steam from a boiler to make its pistons move.

Telecommunications Communications systems that use electricity, radio waves or light to work.

Telegraph A communication system that uses coded pulses of electricity to represent letters and symbols.

Telephone exchange A place where telephone lines meet and can be linked to each other.

Thermionic valve An electronic device contained in a evacuated glass tube.

Transistor A semiconductor device that can act as an electronic switch.

Transmitter A device that gives out signals, such as radio waves.

Turbine A machine that is caused to rotate by a fluid (including liquids and gases such as steam) in order to drive a generator. A gas turbine is another name for a jet engine.

Ultraviolet radiation Invisible radiation similar to light which lies just to the right of visible light on the electromagnetic spectrum.

Vacuum A space that contains nothing, not even air.

Wavelength The distance between two crests or two troughs on a train of waves.

INDEX

Page numbers in **bold** refer to main entries.